The New Achievers

THE NEW ACHIEVERS

Creating a Modern Work Ethic

Perry Pascarella

THE FREE PRESS
A Division of Macmillan, Inc.
NEW YORK

Collier Macmillan Publishers
LONDON

The Free Press
A Division of Macmillan, Inc.
866 Third Avenue, New York, N.Y. 10022

Collier Macmillan Canada, Inc.

Printed in the United States of America

printing number

1 2 3 4 5 6 7 8 9 10

Library of Congress Cataloging in Publication Data

Pascarella, Perry.
    The new achievers.

    Includes bibliographical references and index.
    1. Work ethic.   2. Job satisfaction.   3. Personnel
management.   I. Title.
HD4905.P37   1984   658.3´14   83–49202
ISBN 0–02–924870–1

To Carol, Cindy, and Betsy

Contents ⎯⎯⎯⎯⎯⎯⎯⎯⎯⎯⎯⎯⎯⎯⎯⎯

PART III   MANAGING HUMAN GROWTH

Preface _____

THE CITY LINE FILLING STATION WAS A PLACE where two or three men worked while half a dozen or so were gathered at any time to talk and watch—not working, yet drawn to this center of activity. Some boasted of their working days; others boasted of their schemes for getting by without working. There was, in the air, a mix of admiration both for working and for not working.

Too few people have had an opportunity to invest themselves in the world's work in ways that are of full human value to themselves or others. It is for them that this book is written in the hope that people will become aware of their own potential, their fundamental need to work, and the possibility that the workplace can be a source of fulfillment. I hope, too, that those who manage our workplaces will see that effective management depends on their attention to the human factors and that their success will come, not at the expense of others, but through enriching the lives of others.

The continuous flow of books on management and those on the subject of work generally look at work in the strictly business context. A few plead for humanity without regard for economic realities. I have strived to bring together the economic and the noneconomic aspects of work, dealing with the whole person—including his spiritual dimension.

Discussion of the promise of meaningful work can be more than an expression of wishful thinking today because more and more breakthroughs are occurring in the workplace. There is increasing evidence that companies are going beyond being "nice to people" to genuinely helping them come alive through their work. The conflicting goals of worker and workplace that result in poor quality of product and service are intolerable but not inevitable. By examining both the typical troubled organizations and the exceptional ones, we can learn how to improve the relationship of people to their work. I am inspired by what I have seen and want to hasten the learning process so that more and more people can find richness in their lives.

I am concerned about the millions of unemployed Americans but even more concerned about the work relationship of tens of millions who are employed but working neither to their own nor to others' satisfaction. These employed but unfulfilled workers are the cause of many of our economic and social problems; they suffer the national malaise and personal pain. I am concerned about the loss of personal touch that colors every aspect of our lives. People have been trying to serve economic objectives while denying other, equally compelling needs. Deep down, they want to give something of themselves to the world in exchange for some part in it—some bit of immortality. Unfortunately, too many have been locked out of the opportunity to do so.

It is not my purpose to present gimmicks whereby managers can modify their techniques for attaining just their own economic needs. This is not a "how-to" book but a "how to think" book, as Tom Brown of Honeywell Inc. said after he had studied the barely readable first draft. His yellow circles marked those portions that he especially liked—the first signs that this was a project worth pursuing. The many comments by Mike Badawy of Cleveland State University gave me a better perspective of those points that should be emphasized and raised other considerations to be pursued. Their opinions and their ability to criticize constructively gave me the confidence to proceed. Along the way, Margaret Miner and Frederick Herzberg of the University of Utah, Bob Chitester of Amagin Inc., and Ernesto Poza of E. J. Poza and Associates served as valuable sounding boards. I owe a great deal of thanks to Robert Wallace at The Free Press for seeing the potential in my original proposal and for continually encouraging me to take the time to do something better than I might otherwise have settled for. From her encouragement month after month, to her opinions on logic and clarity in the middle stages of writing, and on to her final checking of spelling and grammar, my wife, Carol, was a partner every step of the way.

The New Achievers

PART I
WORK ETHICS: PAST, PRESENT, AND FUTURE

1

Failing One Another

My barber and i are talking about the tough economic times. Eleven million Americans are on the unemployment rolls. "But a lot of people aren't really working anyway," he says. "You know what I mean?" I nod my head as much as his comb and scissors will permit. But I'm not sure whether he means a lot of people are loafing on the job, or that a lot of people are doing dull, meaningless work. Either way, I would agree.

Some people can't work. Some people won't work. This dual problem was especially troublesome in the early 1980s, when unemployment had become far more extensive than at any time in the memory of most Americans. But it wasn't *the* problem; it was the symptom of a disease caused by people who were employed but not working effectively.

By the early 1980s, the country was on an unhealthy "high"—high prices, high interest rates, high unemployment, a high rate of business failures, and a high level of imported goods. Working Americans suffered cutbacks in their paychecks, and the less fortunate became victims of reductions in government-spending programs.

Spirits were low. Some industries seemed doomed to extinction soon. The auto and steel industries were setting substantially lower sales goals even for the better years ahead; this wiped out many people's hopes of ever regaining employment. Even those persons who were better off felt they were on a sinking ship. They were no longer making the economic gains they once enjoyed; their dollars lacked the power to buy quality goods and services; and they could see the vital supports for a strong economy—such as roads, bridges, and other public facilities—crumbling day by day.

All the safeguards that were to have kept the United States from depression's door had failed to prevent us from slipping into the worst economic slump since World War II. Few people could escape the fear that they were worse off than they had been in previous years and that the future might be even worse.

Even more troublesome than the economic situation itself were people's suspicions about its underlying causes. The economic system wasn't working because not enough people were working as they should. The fascination for consuming goods and leisure-time activities had superheated the economy at one time. Now it seemed to have turned on us by crushing our expectations of further improvement—even of maintaining what we once had. The economic indicators were transmitting a message of something more sinister. We began to suspect that the economic system hadn't failed the people but that the people had somehow failed one another. Painfully, we accepted the possibility that American character might have decayed to a critical state. If this was true, the chances for economic recovery were slim.

For years now, my barber and I and millions of other Americans have been buying products that haven't seemed to meet the old standards; they seem less and less worth the price we are paying for them. Too often, the people selling them to us don't seem to care whether we are pleased with them or even whether we buy them at all. When we need help and attempt to buy services, we often encounter people who don't seem interested in serving us. They are either preoccupied or uninterested. Even when we are ill or injured we have to deal with service agency or hospital staff personnel who are more concerned about their clerical work than their caring work.

The economic malaise seems intertwined with rudeness, disrespect, immorality, crime, and poor government. The economic recession is only part of a more fundamental psychological depression. The total malaise is too pervasive to be the workings of some conspiracy. It is not the scheme of some skillful minority but the accumulation of the wrongdoings of an entire society which, we fear, is inept. Much as some people try to sort out the problems and find their separate causes, my barber and I and others sense that these problems are hopelessly interrelated.

America has lost many of the skills and attitudes needed to be a strong manufacturing nation, and our mounting resentment renders us less and less suited for becoming a service economy. The desire to be served is out of proportion to the willingness and ability to serve. Many of us lack the skill to convey respect for the provider. For every clerk, waiter, or service representative who performs poorly, there is a sizable number of customers who feel no inclination to make a kind remark when they do receive good service.

Many of us have condemned one another for not wanting to work—for not being interested in doing a good job. We fear that the economy has been crippled because so many fellow Americans have been spoiled by affluence and the assumption that they are entitled to certain comforts whether they work for them or not. We have convinced ourselves that the work ethic has been lost and, therefore, that there are no grounds for hoping we can head off decades of further economic decline, social turmoil, and personal pain. If people are coming to the workplace with attitudes and values that make them poor workers, how can we hope to restore our lost economic vitality?

Losing It All

We had it all once, but we feel we are losing it fast. Throughout American history, people had come to expect more and more from their jobs—better pay and more leisure time. The rewards for their efforts were good. Many people were able to find excitement or, at least, escape by consuming an unmatched wealth of goods and services. Pursuing their self interests, Americans had built a fantastic economic machine. But the nation that once had been a super-producer now appears to have pumped itself dry. Frequent recessions, inflation, and the loss of jobs to foreign competitors have brought economic hardships to more and more of us. There is less justification for people to look forward to the automatic improvements in their standard of living or the easy upward mobility they had experienced in the past. Even the most dedicated and skillful workers feel that there is little an individual can do to reverse the ebbing tide of quality and the rising tide of prices.

We have inherited a tradition of steadily improving efficiency. The number of hours of work required to produce a given amount of goods and services has been steadily reduced through most of the nation's history. But in the late 1970s and early 1980s this measure of productivity slipped downward. Failure to improve our productivity—the efficiency with which we convert work, materials, money, and machines into goods and services—means that we cannot improve our standard of living. Failure to improve productivity as fast as other nations means we will lose battle after battle in the world market, and that means losing jobs and falling backwards in our standard of living.

The Human Dimension

There is a third reason for being concerned about poor productivity performance—one not measured by conventional economics. Productivity has human dimensions. It is more than the impersonal relationship of inputs to outputs. It reflects an individual's inventiveness and skills. To be human is to grow, to fight for significance, to distinguish oneself from others. When people cannot contribute to their own material and psychic well-being, they yield to frustration and hostility. When they cannot exert influence on the world around them, they feel less than human. When people are unwilling or unable to work effectively, they suffer the penalties for poor productivity in both economic and very personal, noneconomic terms. Even when they are productive enough to fill their stomachs, they may be unfulfilled in other ways.

We, the people, are both the victims and the cause of the productivity problem. Politicians and economists attack the economic problems with "hard" economic solutions, dealing with such things as tax incentives, interest rates, and levels of investment in plants and equipment. Round after round of economic and political remedies have failed to cool the American fever because the cause is not "the economy." We, the people, determine how productive we are in the use of our resources, of which we are the principal one. Manipulating the hard factors will not correct or compensate for human wrongdoings and weaknesses. How can we expect someone else to deliver expiation for our sins? We have developed a gut feeling that we are victims of our own complacency, carelessness, laziness, and selfishness. We may assume it's not our own but the other guy's fault. He deserves trouble. We smolder with resentment because we have to share his fate.

Tax cuts, government welfare programs, import quotas and other political "solutions" can address only part of America's productivity problem. They will not solve the problems of people and people relationships. They will not reverse negative attitudes toward work or change work so that it meets people's expectations. Economic policies can only enhance the efforts of productive people. Government programs to reduce unemployment won't work when misuse of the employed—or underemployment—is the culprit.

Economic failure has been accomplishing what preaching and moralizing have not been able to do; it has sensitized us to the possibility that our values and our organizations are not sustainable in a changing world. Some people believe that industrialized economies carry the seeds of their own destruction. Our economic malaise and unmet human needs come as no surprise to them. Emphasis on consumption eventually weakens people's productive capability, they say. As it engenders values that create an increasing demand for the products of the system, it robs people of the ability to produce them. If this line of thinking is being proved in modern America, can we hope to restore our industrial strength?

An even more troublesome question arises in the minds of some: If industrial systems create unproductive, materialistic people, should we really want to restore the system? Should we, instead, search for a way to dismantle the structures of our system and revert to some simpler, better way of life?

Restoring People

Attaining success in both economic and noneconomic terms will require more than modifying or undoing the system's structures, however. It must begin with restoring people both as individuals and as members of the human community. In *An Immodest Agenda*, Amitai Etzioni points out the danger of blaming all our malaise on government and assuming that individuals would step forward to restore an energetic nation if government involvements were reduced.[1] Etzioni questions whether Americans are ready to stand on their own. They have been robbed of their individual initiative, and the natural community that would support individual action has been displaced by formal structures. The heavy intervention of government in people's lives has acted as a double-edged sword, wounding both the individual and the natural community.

In the late 1970s, Christopher Lasch, in *The Culture of Narcissism*, wrote that Americans were not simply the victims of affluence but had been made helpless by the many third-party organizations and specialists who do things for them.[2] These mechanisms, designed for smoothing the rough spots of life, have replaced human contact and personal involvement in our lives.

The more economic progress Americans have made, the more they have delegated noneconomic matters to institutions and left only an economic box for the individual to occupy. They paid someone else, directly or through taxes, to perform human acts that they didn't care to undertake themselves. The prevailing attitude became, "Let the schools do all the teaching, the hospitals care for the sick, the insurance companies pay for damages, the psychiatrists deal with people's frustrations." In effect, people sold themselves piece by piece, narrowing the definition of what it means to be human.

Today's business, social, and political institutions make people feel more and more helpless. The individual frequently can neither exercise his own initiative nor rely on institutional help to get something done in a satisfactory manner. Whether it's repairing one's car, getting medical care, or protecting oneself from crime, the individual often feels he or she can't do the job alone and can find no effective help. Helplessness leads to frustration, and frustration leads to further helplessness. The box gets smaller and smaller.

Some people are trying to break through the artificial limitations imposed on them. Sometimes, they assert their humanity positively; they go into business for themselves so they can do things their way or they learn new skills so they can get a better job. Others assert themselves negatively; they evade work on the job or they go to the extreme of injuring people or property. The challenge in the years ahead will be to direct this force toward individual and societal good.

In the 1960s and 1970s, a liberal challenge to the system, ironically, resulted in enlarging the system to take care of more individuals in more ways. With the dawning of the 1980s, a conservative trend in American social and political sentiments challenged the system by attempting to strip away some of the supports and programs. Included in the conservative swing were those who fought for the opportunity to allow for greater self-reliance. But Etzioni asks the critical question: If we were to get government out of business and our personal lives, would the individual come forth and do better?

It is doubtful that any overnight change would unleash a nation of individuals ready to operate more effectively than they are now under the controls, incentives, and guidance of government. Rather than the emergence of a healthy combination of self-reliance and community action, we might see a surge of senseless individualism that would block social and economic progress. Neither greater nor less government involvement, then, seems in itself to be central to the solution of the troubles gnawing at Americans.

Yet, if we look carefully, we can see around us today people grasping for ways to build a wholeness of self and to find a place in some greater unity—the neighborhood, the work group, the planet, the universe, or a supreme being. Perhaps at no time in man's history have people been so insistent on pursuing their search for meaning and significance. We are moving toward a "self-realization ethic," says futurist Willis Harman.[3] We are beginning to fashion a "self-development ethic," says psychoanalyst Michael Maccoby.[4] And after studying the results of many surveys—his own and others'—of American attitudes and values, social analyst Daniel Yankelovich suspects we are moving toward an "ethic of commitment."[5] These analysts, too, are saying that people are trying to break through the tight definition that has been imposed on them. People are turning inward, reaching outward, and looking upward. The drive toward personal growth leads many to commitment to things outside themselves. For some, too, this means seeking a spiritual or transcendental connection.

The genuine searching for meaningful self-development is accompanied by random, undirected, irresponsible assertion of self on the part of some individuals who have not developed the values and skills that can lead them to meaningful lives as individuals and as members of society. What is worse, we seem to lack a vehicle for nurturing such values and skills.

Where can people look for help? If not to government, then to whom? Etzioni urges us to restore the family and the schools—the traditional vehicles for nurturing positive human values.[6] Much as I agree with his sentiments and hear his plea, I cannot hope that a plea will lift despondent people to action. Restoring the family and the schools is, unfortunately, too big an objective in itself to be a solution to the problems at hand.

The family has been on the decline in its influence on American values. The mobility of working parents has removed their children from the influence of aunts, uncles, and grandparents. Instability of marriage itself has left millions of children with one or no full-time parent close by. Modern life-styles put children in touch with numerous influences that rival those of whatever family they have. At the same time, the schools have stepped farther and farther away from the values business. Lost in the attempt to prepare people for roles in the economic system, they have done less and less to teach or reinforce any particular values.

A Vehicle for Change

This would indeed be a time for complete despair if there were not some vehicle to support personal development, providing the means for self-expression in ways that are constructive both for the individual and for society. But such a vehicle is beginning to have a positive impact. The business corporation is now making the first significant moves toward helping individuals realize their potential and enabling them to grow to their full measure. While further decline in the effectiveness of the family and school in shaping values is quite likely for some time to come, we can already see signs of people coming alive at work, acquiring life skills, and proceeding toward personal growth.

There are three propositions that can give us cause for renewed hope in restoring the individual and providing direction for individual action and social policy:

1. The work ethic is very much alive.
2. The business corporation can be the primary vehicle for nurturing positive human values and developing skills that will help people lead more fulfilling lives.
3. We need a new view of what it means to be human and the role that work plays in our humanity if we are to attend to both our economic and our noneconomic needs.

Meeting people's full range of needs runs counter to what the corporation has generally done for people and what people all too often expect of themselves. The rise of industrialization led to a narrow definition of man as an economic unit. In the earlier stages of the industrial era, the individual was reduced to an interchangeable part in highly structured work situations. In effect, the individual was eliminated as a consideration.

In recent times, work has been made a little less hazardous, a little less physically demanding, but often less and less intellectually challenging and individually rewarding. Sadly enough, not all people want to be challenged. They reject stimulation and challenge despite the pains of boredom and loneliness. They try to invest as little of themselves as possible to ward off boredom without going beyond a point of equilibrium. Work often gets in the way of what people are striving for in life, providing either too little or too much challenge. It forces some people to surrender the companionship they can find

:. It forces others into more per-

irhood bar, taking time out for a
ices may scoff at the suggestion
:le for nurturing human values,
ing them develop skills for better
doubt that life has any meaning,
: concept of human growth. The
s the best they hope for at work.
work to be nothing more than a
eant sacrifice rather than gain.
;reat or too small, the mismatch
id what the individual demands
rives a sense of failure.
ild enough to innovate job struc-
cipate in decision making have
: view of people pays off, not only
By building networks of decision
irder followers, they are produc-
ithusiasm to carry out those deci-
i that the work ethic is dead. For
poration can be a vehicle for hu-
/ neither sacrificing economic ob-
they are attaining both economic
power and human growth. They see that the two go hand in hand.

Workers fortunate enough to be in such new work situations are learning with management to reduce distrust and to cooperate since both parties realize that their economic fate is tied together. One auto worker told me: "We don't care how long the problems existed in this plant or who is to blame. We realize now that we have to work together if we want to stay in business." In more and more workplaces, employees are enjoying a sense of victory rather than defeat and surrender. As others observe this taking place, they will find that there is more to life than they had expected. The press operator, the diemaker, the salesclerk—all can take an active part in the business rather than feeling merely that they are being acted upon.

Corporate efforts to nurture positive values and become involved in human development will often have to overcome the resistance of the very people who would benefit from it. They themselves assume the "work ethic" is dead. Many business managers would be included among those who would scoff at the assertion that the work ethic is

alive and that people can make a real contribution to solving corporate problems. They are caught in the middle between unhappy
customers and unhappy workers. They feel the same frustrations as
the rest of us plus the special agony of trying to keep their organizations afloat. They are inclined to believe that economic improvement
depends on developing better and better systems of control and eliminating the human factor wherever possible since people are coming
to the workplace with negative attitudes toward work.

Having heard the situation discussed from both the management
and nonmanagement points of view, I have found that many managers see the worker as the chief stumbling block for the improvement of goods and services. Those workers who are concerned about
doing a quality job, on the other hand, see the manager and management systems as their biggest restraint. All too often, management
views the worker as self-indulgent and rebellious—a carryover from
the 1960s. Workers, as well as the public at large, hold a nineteenth-
century view of the corporation.

If we could peel away layers of misperceptions, false teachings,
and unrealistic expectations, we would find that the work ethic is still
very much alive. Despite the changing values swirling around us, we
would discover that people have numerous reasons for wanting to
work. We would see the makings of a strong, new, self-development
ethic which has a producer—rather than a consumer—orientation.
People's new perceptions of themselves and their intensifying fight
for significance and fulfillment do not mesh well with the economic
system, however. They do not lead to good work behavior in conventional terms. They do not fit the old notion of what a "work ethic" is.

The corporation must develop, rather than restrain, the individual in order to elicit greater commitment and creativity in the
struggle to improve productivity and product quality. That means
creating winners, not losers. We have reached a stage of industrialization that requires greater—not less—human input. Despite
the mechanization going on in both goods-producing and service industries, more and more human touch, creativity, and dedication to
detail are necessary for the corporation to succeed. This need coin-
cides with growing insistence by some people that they be permitted
to invest more of their human powers in the workplace. Since industrialization has reached a point where continuation of the dehumanizing trend in the workplace makes the organization a loser as
well, further economic advance depends on reversing the dehumanizing process.

Members of the corporation, from top to bottom, are beginning to realize that the values that lead to personal growth are the very ones that generate economic growth in this point in United States industrial evolution. We are, then, at a stage where efforts to integrate economic and human considerations will be intensified. Industrialization will become a humanizing endeavor rather than the dehumanizing process it has often been in the past.

Despite all the scorn heaped upon the business corporation, it is here of all places that we can look for the first steps in restoring American character. The workplace will increasingly become the place to nurture the very values that were once surrendered there. It will respond to the struggle by both managers and nonmanagers to make meaningful achievements. As it empowers more and more people to fulfill themselves, it will, in turn, be made a more powerful producer of goods and services by the growing number of new achievers.

The Response to Change

Leadership in the workplace will increasingly become dedicated to people development—not molding people to fit the organization, but enabling each individual to fulfill himself or herself. Management will lead some people to their first awareness that there is such a thing as human growth. It will enable members of the organization to move toward fulfillment by providing the proper job structure, work assignments, training, and environment for growth. Then it will have to respond to people's broadening range of skills and interests and to their deepening commitment.

People have been failing one another, and they have been failing themselves. They have been coming together in the workplace—sometimes reluctantly—to meet their material needs. But there are many other needs to be met by work. In the following chapters we will examine these forces that constitute a work ethic despite the many obituaries written about it. We will examine how the workplace and workers have changed in ways that thwart the conversion of this ethic into positive work behavior.

It is essential to understand the wave of changing values as well as some timeless truths because managers who accept traditional, negative assumptions about people are not going to be the winners in the decades ahead. And workers who expect only the traditional rewards in the workplace will miss the opportunity for personal development and fulfillment. As a nation, we might continue the futile search for a strictly economic strategy for our economic problems and a strictly noneconomic route to human growth; we could press on, not realizing that these objectives are bound together. There can be no significant economic advance without consideration of human growth and fulfillment, and there can be little human growth without attention to the economic aspects of life.

2

Not by Bread Alone

"WITH THREE KIDS TO FEED, I have to have a job."

"I have to work at least part time to help the family make ends meet."

"I gotta make a living."

The financial rewards of working seem to overshadow all others. Early industrial man worked for economic survival, and financial compensation is still the common denominator of people's expectations when they are employed. However, we should not allow the reason people generally accept the available jobs today to obscure the many other reasons that make it natural and essential for people to perform work and demand even more from it than they have in the past.

The financial aspect is so fundamental to civilized man's concept of work that it has distorted our understanding of the meaning of work and the meaning of what it is to be human. This common denominator, which reduces our view of humankind to a narrow, economic one, leads us to assume that man is merely an animal that must be sustained: A consuming mechanism that must somehow obtain the wherewithal to purchase goods and services—not only for survival, but beyond that, to compensate for the pains of being alive.

This line of thinking leads to schemes for providing people incomes regardless of what kind of work they are performing or whether they have a job, and it scarcely considers their need to find

15

some of the joys that can come from the tasks they perform, the learning experienced in their work, and their relationships with other people. It distracts us from considering the many potential "incomes" that a person might derive from performing work.

Many people have been deprived of such incomes. They have seldom, if ever, seen beyond the economic dimension of work. Throughout their lives, the messages they have received about work from family, friends, fellow workers, and even supervisors has been a negative one. They have, understandably, not looked to the workplace to offer anything more.

In order to appreciate what the fruits of work might be, we have to consider what it means to be human—what the range of man's needs is. A widely accepted view of what drives human behavior was laid out in the 1940s by psychologist Abraham Maslow when he described five sets of needs and arranged them into a hierarchy.[1] The most fundamental or lowest level of needs—the physiological—has to do with survival; it includes the body's need for food and drink.

When an individual's physiological needs are sufficiently met to permit his attention and energies to be devoted to other pursuits, he or she then tends to safety needs, which include the search for orderliness, familiar patterns, and organization. When these needs, in turn, are under control, an individual will strive to meet the need for love; he or she will seek the affection of and the sense of belongingness with others.

Next, said Maslow, comes the need for esteem from oneself and from others. He established two groupings of needs within this level of the hierarchy: the need for strength, achievement, adequacy, independence, and freedom; the need for attention, appreciation, and recognition. At the fifth level of needs—self-actualization—an individual does what he feels he is best fitted for, he strives to be all that he can be with his particular talents and limitations.

As the lowest level of need is essentially met, a person will then begin responding to the next higher level, Maslow believed. A starving person will struggle first to feed himself; he will abandon attempts to meet other needs until that one is reasonably, but not necessarily completely, satisfied. Likewise, Maslow reasoned, the self-actualizing person must have essentially met all the other levels of needs; he cannot ignore them.

Early man responded to the first level of needs—survival. His work was directed almost entirely to obtaining food and protecting himself from nature. Civilized man simplified the meeting of survival needs and began tending to safety and belonging needs as he brought

order and organization into his life. Industrial man was able to respond to the need for belonging and esteem as the financial rewards
for his work exceeded his survival and safety needs and could be used
to purchase goods or experiences that would win the admiration of
others. Although his work was sometimes alienating, the work scene
either provided some sense of community or the financial means to
find attachments and identity outside the job.

For some people, work has been practically their only source of
identity and companionship. Dulling as their tasks may be, they have
prided themselves in doing the best they know how because the
workplace has been not just a place to be but a community. On the
job, they joke, complain, tell stories, recount baseball games, and do
the many other small things that give them a sense of belonging. Off
the job, they use their economic rewards to win the esteem of others;
money and the things it can buy sometimes bring recognition and
even admiration.

In the 1950s, psychologist Frederick Herzberg analyzed aspects
of the work situation and their influence on work behavior.[2] There
are certain factors that can provide satisfaction, the principal ones
being achievement, recognition, challenging work, responsibility,
and advancement, he found. When these factors are present, a person will be motivated to perform well. On the other hand, factors
such as company policy, supervision, pay, working conditions, and
relations with others in the workplace have the potential of causing
dissatisfaction. If these dissatisfiers are attended to properly, job
dissatisfaction can be minimized. They cannot, however, be managed
or manipulated to create motivation. Herzberg, therefore, labeled
them "hygiene" factors. Motivation depends on the other set of factors—the "satisfiers."

Throughout his years of writing, from the 1950s to the present,
Herzberg has lamented that management tends to deal with the hygiene factors and mistakenly expects people to respond as satisfied,
motivated workers. In order to engage a person's inherent motivators, he says, management has to structure the work so that it offers
something to which the worker can commit himself and through
which he can grow personally—in short, a "love" relationship with
the work process or the product.

Herzberg's motivation-hygiene theory was supported by psychological research, but it was based on a philosophical concept: the
duality of man. It takes into account the traditional struggle between
man the animal and man the human. The dissatisfiers—or Maslow's
physiological and safety needs, and perhaps the need for belong-

ing—are shared by man and other animals. The motivators—the need for esteem and self-actualization—however, are special qualities of humans.

Feeling Special

The human animal is caught in the struggle between two worlds. He tries to assert himself as something unique and is simultaneously pulled back into the fold with his fellow animals. "This is the paradox: he is out of nature and hopelessly in it . . . ," said psychologist Ernest Becker.[3] Dependent as he is on his bonds to the physical world, he maintains that "ache of cosmic specialness."[4]

To understand a person, therefore, it is essential to understand not only what he appears to be but what he insists on struggling to be. In industrialized work up to now, however, people have not been able to explore what they might become. They have all too often been able to win only economic means for satisfying their survival and safety needs. Some meet their belonging needs by feeling that they are doing their part in performing some small bit of the world's work. Sometimes, they meet this need in the comradeship of fellow workers in those moments when they are not actually working.

Generally, people have had to turn outside the workplace to find esteem and fulfilling experiences and relationships. Some jobs do provide opportunities to do that—some positions in the academic community, the professions, management, and other knowledge-based occupations, for example. The less defined the job, the greater the opportunity for the individual to grow and to search for self-definition and fulfillment. But many jobs are fairly tightly defined. People with a strong drive for self-actualization may, therefore, resort to demanding relatively high economic income from their jobs so they will have the means to pursue their quest in nonwork settings. The young engineer who is assigned dull, repetitive work at the drawing board, for example, may do barely passable work and cut corners on the hours spent in the office so he can build a boat on his own time.

With greater economic security provided by the system, more schooling, and greater mobility, those who are earnestly seeking fulfillment, as well as those who are seeking escape, may reject what they find at work. Experienced managers have seen workers refuse to do what they're told when they did not at first understand why they were doing it. Workers seem less interested in the rules and more interested in the purpose of the work they are being told to do.

Few are likely to do things simply because someone says they ought to.

During the World Future Society assembly in Washington in 1982, Barbara Marx Hubbard, founder of the Futures Network, and I discussed our views on work while crowding in a quick lunch. She commented that she no longer is at the "ought to" stage; she does things because they are fulfilling. "It's the pleasure principle at a higher level," she laughed. We agreed that attending a meeting where we could discuss life's big questions with some of the world's best thinkers was so exciting and challenging that it was difficult to call what we were doing "work." But it is our kind of work. "It's sublime work," she said.

There may be a fine line between loafing and sublime work, but there is a significant difference between working because one ought to and working because one wants to. Most people who have worked have never suspected that work could be sublime. They haven't been aware of their potential to develop or to self-actualize, particularly at work. Work has taught them to feel like losers. Yet, work is where people try to prove their worth to themselves or to others. Rightly or wrongly, they may measure their worth in terms of whether they are employed, who employs them and in what capacity or at what rate of pay. They take identity from such things.

Many people do sense that certain other individuals are getting more from their work than the satisfaction of minimal requirements. They do not, however, expect that they themselves will satisfy these higher, individual needs. They look only for the social "income" that can be derived from work. To work is to be part of society's work. Work is "where it's at." Whether it's the bustle of the big city at lunchtime or the relaxed atmosphere of a small-town factory, the workplace is where one can be part of something. It is where people engage in the activities that make the world go round—baking bread, assembling cars, floating bonds, cutting hair, and so on. For some, work means being directly involved in the action. For others, it is at least being *near* the action—a chance to be associated with those people who *are* doing the meaningful things. For many of us, work is vital for its human contact.

Mixed Motives

Not all of us are driven by the same needs. Herzberg has provided archetypes of successive waves of new entrants into the workforce that help us appreciate the changes in workers' predominant needs and values over the years.[5] He says the "external immigrants" made up most of the workforce from colonial times until World War II. They came from foreign shores to work in America. They accepted inequality and expected to fit into a hierarchy, says Herzberg. They could see the significance of the work they did; many of them built bridges, railways, and skyscrapers. No matter how humble their individual roles, they were part of something great and they felt it. They believed in hard work and thrift.

Following World War II, "organization man" immigrants typified a key new element in the workforce. Seeking the security and high living offered by the big organization, as depicted in William H. Whyte's book *The Organization Man*, their "structures" were the organizations themselves. These workers often couldn't see the product of their efforts, says Herzberg, but they were concerned with career. They surrendered their family responsibilities to the church and the schools.

In the 1960s came the "internal immigrants"—women and minority groups—who had been in this society but who had been locked out of the better jobs. They wanted everything they had been denied, says Herzberg. They were looking for personal significance, and they wanted it quickly.

Today, we find all of these elements in the American workplace. We have a mixed workforce, looking for a variety of rewards. Old management practices won't work for all of them. The traditional incentives to get people to work—money, fear, sense of duty—are not effective for nearly half of today's workforce, said Daniel Yankelovich in the late 1970s.[6] The old carrot-and-stick incentives don't suit the "turned off" workers who comprise about one-fourth of the workforce. These people are poorly educated, and they respond to sensations. The traditional incentives are also ineffective for a quite different one-sixth of the workforce whom Yankelovich calls "middle management." These youthful, white-collar, managerial or professional, college-educated workers have the strongest creativity and achievement needs. They hunger for responsibility, challenge, autonomy, and informality; they want something vital to which to commit themselves.

According to Yankelovich, traditional incentives are still effective for the "go-getters": These are the young, ambitious, sales types who are attracted by money and status. These incentives also suit the "work-before-pleasure" employees who tend to be older, dedicated, and see money as less important than the work itself. And, of course, they work for the "habitual worker" who is not looking for meaning but for structure, job security, guidance, and clear responsibilities.

There is no single ideal job or ideal reward for American workers. Some people are satisfied with the job that doesn't demand much of them; they prefer to have the work routine thought out for them. They don't want to move to a different machine or sell a different line of goods. Others may be frustrated by undemanding jobs; they want to excel and sometimes feel the organization gets in their way. They may have what they think are great ideas for doing things better or faster, but they're blocked by the need to "go through channels." They may lack the supplies needed to maintain a fast pace of production, or they may find that so many procedures are spelled out in company policy that they cannot add any variation or improvements to the job.

Population trends suggest that we will have more and more workers who want to exercise discretion on the job. At the same time, the number of work-before-pleasure and habitual workers who generally accept unchallenging work (and even regard it as honorable to do what one ought to do) is declining.

In 1983, Yankelovich reported that in a survey of 845 American jobholders, 52 percent expressed a strong form of work ethic: "I have an inner need to do the very best job possible, regardless of pay." Another 21 percent expressed a more limited commitment: "I find my work interesting, but I wouldn't let it interfere with the rest of my life." Only one out of four expressed older concepts of work such as "one of life's unpleasant necessities" or "a business transaction."[7]

Even in the recession years of the early 1980s, people who were beginning careers sought employment with companies that had a reputation of offering an opportunity for self-fulfillment. They, as well as those who were seeking job changes, could not find all the challenging jobs they wanted, however.

People who are responding to the upper levels of needs are better matched to work as it is likely to be in the future, but they are victims of the predominant work content, structure, and rewards of yesterday and today. Increasingly, people are testing their worth in new ways that are meaningful to them in terms of their self-development and sense of self-worth. A fast-rising percentage of women, for example, is entering the workforce. While the majority of them do so because of economic necessity as either primary or secondary breadwinners, many are in the workforce as more than jobholders; they are pursuing *careers*. They are proving themselves as persons, seeking self-fulfillment through the resources and reinforcements for growth that are found in the workplace. Housework or child-rearing are vital roles, but they seldom match the workplace in giving recognition or the opportunity to learn new skills. In one study, the overwhelming majority—87 percent—of working women polled cited "personal sense of accomplishment" as the main reason they were working.[8]

Negative View

Although America's industrial structure has been undergoing some major shifts, most jobs are essentially like those of earlier industrial times. To a large extent they are built on a negative view or, at best, a narrow economic view of people. The negative view was well described more than twenty years ago by Douglas McGregor.[9] Noting that some managers are pessimistic about people while others are optimistic, he found that the two groups hold differing assumptions about people. The negative view, which McGregor called "Theory X," is based on the assumption that people are lazy, avoid responsibility, and don't care about the organization. "Theory Y" managers, on the other hand, believe that even when a person acts lazy, he or she is not naturally inclined to do so. McGregor was urging managers to realize that people seek responsibility, are capable of self-direction, and can care about an organization and be committed to it.

Theory X management was tolerated by the external immigrant, the work-before-pleasure person, and the habitual worker, but Theory Y better meets the mixed workforce of today. Because the Theory X manager tries to modify people and standardize them, he collides with the individual's drive to be nonstandard. The Theory Y manager appreciates the fact that people differ from one another and tries to learn how to modify the situation so that each person will respond with the maximum application of his or her talents.

Obtaining the maximum response depends on individualizing the challenge presented to a worker and the amount of creativity and involvement expected of him. Management's challenge is to approach each individual on that person's level of need. Traditionally, however, management has not lifted its sights beyond the economic view of people. It has dealt primarily with the physiological needs—especially the financial. Workers traditionally have demanded more and more of these returns to compensate for their unsatisfied psychic needs. But financial compensation cannot truly compensate for the personal sacrifices. As people have become more and more aware of what they are sacrificing, they have tried to lessen the sacrifice and increase the "compensation." They have demanded more and more pay for less and less work. The number of years worked over a person's career and the number of hours worked per year have fallen dramatically in recent decades.

At the same time, workers are less hesitant to voice their demands. Fear of unemployment no longer silences protests as effectively as it once did. With welfare supports, more than one wage earner in many households, and the virtual disappearance of the stigma of not being employed, people are not easily forced to the workplace. What is more important, and perhaps less obvious, is the fact that they cannot be forced to the levels of productivity and dedication to quality that today's employers need.

Heroic Defiance

All man's needs taken together destine him to be a producer. Inclined to be a solver of problems and a changer of the conditions in which he finds himself, man departs from his fellow animals to become a doer. Work, therefore, singles him out as something special. "Man," said Ernest Becker, "is the one animal who is implacably driven to work beyond animal needs precisely because he is not a secure animal." He is driven by "the urge to stand out as a hero, to transcend the limitations of the human condition and achieve victory over impotence and finitude."[10] This is the stuff that philosophers and theologians speak of when they refer to the "dignity" or "nobility" of work.

Numerous studies in recent years have shown that workers want recognition for their skills and accomplishment, feedback that tells them when they have accomplished something that someone else values, some "say" in the decisions that affect their work, and the opportunity to develop new skills or acquire new knowledge. They may not be deliberately asking for "nobility" in their work, but this is, beneath it all, what they want. We all need a dignity of purpose that we can take into the center of our lives.

Work should be central to people's lives since it has the potential of meeting so many needs, but the negative, strictly economic view of work has often robbed it of that capability. When a person is forced into the nine-to-five syndrome which involves only part of him, he is left with little choice but to seek self-fulfillment off the job. But empty jobs reinforce empty lives and often lead people to engage in leisure-time activities—or nonactivities—that are not fulfilling. People who accept dull work need extraordinary self-discipline to do better than spend their leisure time watching television or drinking beer to pass the time.

People need what they are more likely to find in sports or war—victories that enable them to steal a bit of significance and perhaps a bit of immortality. Life is a battle to assert control over the conditions into which we have been plunged simply by being alive. To varying degrees, we are all affected by the fact that we are not fully in control and that we have to live with illusion as well as reality. Some people try to influence the forbidding world; others try to escape it. Some attain a measure of what they need by involving themselves in the work of the world. Others hold to themselves, resisting any growth experiences and committing as little as possible of themselves. Unfortunately, in our design of work, we have leaned more toward allowing people to escape than to plunge boldly into the battle. We have not addressed the fundamental truth regarding the individual's struggle to be a hero—to achieve some victory—to exert some influence over his environment.

We find in the workplace both the dreamer who is thwarted by the limitations put on his efforts and the nondreamer who expects to exchange very little in his work contract. Those who are highly motivated may find too little room in the job to grow. Those who suffer from the lack of a dream, the inability to dream, or the conviction that their dreams could not possibly be realized seek nothing in the work itself. This is the sad lot of those unskilled, unmotivated people we call "unemployable." Some people are pained by the potential of their humanity; others suffer the loss of humanity without knowing it—without realizing what they are failing to become. Both the dreamers and the nondreamers need help in setting and attaining goals whereby they can be victorious. They need direction and purpose—something to believe in and work toward. Unfortunately, our workplaces are, by and large, not organized for dealing with dreams.

Ethics of Work

Work, therefore, presents moral issues. But we have not attended to them. Although we may quickly become concerned about anyone who strives for income without working or who does a job poorly, we ignore the other moral considerations having to do with work. We allow people to work *only* for money. We offer only mindless tasks for those who would try to escape confrontation with life, and we encourage their being distracted or pacified through the consumption of goods and services. We don't question the purpose of the activities of the person who is "all wrapped up" in his or her work. Long-time student of labor Robert Schrank points out, "What tends to get lost from Maslow's schema and its application to the workplace is the moral issue that asks: What does my creativity create? What is the impact of my self-actualization beyond me?"[11] Actually, Maslow wrote a great deal about the social and religious response or the searching that a person goes through when he is self-actualizing. The upper levels of needs take the individual beyond himself to both social and spiritual considerations, Maslow believed.

Our concept of what we are determines what we expect from work; we attach obligations to work according to what we see of ourselves and our purpose. Work becomes a matter of "ought to," and an ethic of work arises. This work ethic may be a social one leading people to work for the good of the group, or it may be the obligation to work for the fulfillment of one's own needs. Man has worked under various moral justifications for his efforts throughout history. Major religions have advanced spiritual imperatives for work. Judaism, Catholicism, and Protestantism shaped a particularly American work ethic that once spurred people to work for the glory of God.

Today, there seems to be no consensus as to what the ethics of work are. We hear of the "Protestant ethic," the "Puritan ethic," or simply the "old work ethic." The transcendental dimension to our work has been lost. When we lament the loss of the old ethic we are perhaps expressing not so much a concern for people who might be damned by not working as a selfish concern—"it's a damn shame people won't work as we would like them to."

Because we have stripped the moral considerations from our view of work, we limit people's ability to be fully human. Work "is a fundamental dimension of man's existence on earth," says Pope John Paul II. In a 1981 encyclical, he stressed the centrality of work to being human.[12] Alluding to God's order to man to subdue the earth and have dominion over all living things (Gen. 1:28), he reasoned: "From the beginning therefore he is called to work."[13] In a time of widespread unemployment throughout the world, Pope John Paul II was looking beyond the economic need for work. "[If the solution of] the social question, which keeps coming up and becomes ever more complex, must be sought in the direction of 'making life more human,' then the key, namely human work, acquires fundmental and decisive importance," he wrote.[14]

Work may have lost its spiritual aspect in the eyes of many, but people haven't lost their spiritual dimension. We overlook the fact that work, in its fullest sense, should allow for people's spiritual strivings. Beyond the satisfaction of material needs, beyond the needs of society, work should enable each individual to pursue his or her search for meaning and significance. In the years ahead, as more and more people seek work that responds to their ethic of self-fulfillment and commitment to others, they will insist on examining their spiritual dimension.

3

What Happened to the Old Protestant Ethic?

AN INDIVIDUAL COMES TO WORK to meet economic needs, belonging needs, the need to feel a sense of self-worth, the need to serve others, or the need for self-development and self-expression—any or all in their many shades. He or she may respond to different needs at different times. In earlier times, the reason for working was more clear-cut: economic necessity reinforced by a moral imperative.

The need to earn a living still drives people to seek a job, but work no longer seems to have that same transcendental connection for many Americans. It is impossible to measure the religious commitment of a society at any point in time and make a sound comparison with some time in the past; however, there is little doubt that religion is playing a lesser role in our public lives today than in early America and during the early years of industrialization. In the past two or three decades, the nation has become highly sensitized to any laws, regulations, or national policies—extant or proposed—that would bring church and state closer together. Religious beliefs, or the absence of them, are protected by barring discussion of religious or moral considerations in the official public arena.

Americans still consider themselves religious, however. Regardless of their church affiliation or nonaffiliation, regardless of the degree to which their daily lives are governed by transcendent considerations, they believe in a god, they say. In a study of American values done for the Connecticut Mutual Life Insurance Co., 94 percent of adults said they occasionally feel God loves them; 73 percent feel that frequently.[1] Although only 44 percent of these people attend church regularly, 73 percent consider themselves "religious."

Other studies have shown, year after year, that over 90 percent of Americans believe in God but that fewer than 50 percent regularly attend worship services. There is little evidence, then, that most Americans are deeply and continuously influenced by the religious word. In fact, the analysts working on the Connecticut Mutual study call only one-fourth of the respondents "highly religious."

Religious commitment may no longer be the all-embracing force it once was, but the Connecticut Mutual report's authors conclude that it is still the "strongest predictor" of a person's satisfaction and involvement with his or her work. Of the most religious respondents to the survey, nearly all feel dedicated to their work while only two-thirds of the "least religious" feel that way.

Although religion may influence some people's attitudes toward work today, we are far from reaching a consensus on any of the troublesome questions that would be provided answers by a common ideology of work. There is little agreement about the relationship of work to life's purpose, of individual interests versus those of the community, or of working to perfect life here on earth versus relying on God's salvation. There is disagreement not only between "religious" and not-so-religious persons but even within the ranks of those with strong religious beliefs.

The effect of differing spiritual views on people's attitudes toward work was revealed in a survey done for the Continental Group.[2] A high correlation appeared among those who engage in traditional religious activities, those who believe in giving a high priority to economic growth, and those who place a high priority on work that makes a contribution to society. We might call this the more traditional view of economic growth and the meaning of work. On the other hand, there is a growing number of people who favor more cautious economic growth and who give a high priority to preserving the earth's resources. People in this group are likely to regard themselves as "driven" individuals. They tend to be less content with their work situations and more aggressive in demanding that their expectations be met. We have, then, at least two work ethics shaping people's behavior. One leads its adherents to accept traditional work structures and rewards while the other leads to resistance.

Money and Morals

In early America there was an obvious need to work for one's economic survival and a dominant moral obligation to work as well. This obligation was the basis for what is referred to as the "Protestant ethic" or "Puritan ethic." The blend of economic necessity—for the individual and the community—and the moral force weaved its way through much of American history. In time, however, this fabric became unraveled. Why?

Two powerful and competing movements laid the ideological foundation for American life: the Reformation and the Enlightenment. Both were reactions against the traditional church. Both carried strong messages regarding the individual in relation to the universe, his work, and his wealth.

The Reformation began with Martin Luther (1483–1546) challenging the notion that individual salvation could be earned through good works as prescribed by the church. Salvation could come only through God's grace, said Luther. While the Roman Church had an "elect"—the priests—Luther and other Protestant leaders taught that the "elect" could be anyone. Anyone, but not all. John Calvin (1509–1564) said that those who would be granted salvation had already been predetermined. Material success, he allowed, is a sign that one has been designated by God for salvation.

Luther saw no particular virtue or evil in poverty. "God does not condemn the possession of wealth, but the evil use of it, that is, its use merely to satisfy one's selfish desire. . . ."[3] Man is in the world to be of service to his fellow man and to God, said Luther. A person who conducts himself accordingly will not lose his heart to wealth and will use his riches for the good of all, he believed. He advanced the revolutionary concept of a worldy "calling"—the keystone of what was to become the Protestant work ethic. Prior to that, in the teachings of the Roman Church, the highest calling had been the monastic life of contemplation. But Luther's "calling" was to action in the secular world as an expression of brotherly love. ". . . this moral justification of worldy activity was one of the most important results of the Reformation," wrote Max Weber, the German sociologist, in his classic book *The Protestant Ethic and the Spirit of Capitalism.*[4]

For many centuries, man had regarded work as a curse. For early Hebrews, it was atonement for original sin. For early Christians, "labor" or "toil" was not something to be pursued with all one's energies. But Luther and Calvin brought significance to work. They presented it as the bridge between heaven and earth.

Calvin went one step further in drawing man into worldly activity for spiritual purpose. He preached "maximum effort"; when a person produces more than he needs, said Calvin, this surplus should not be wasted on personal appetites. It should serve the glory of God by being reinvested to improve one's work and provide even greater surpluses for the glory of God.[5] For centuries, Christianity had condemned profit-making; but early Protestantism supported a profound social and economic shift. Wealth had long been associated with oppressors; now it was taken as a sign that one was among God's elect.

Early Lutheranism and Calvinism coincided with secular, economic changes that were occurring in Europe. People were rising above the subsistence level. A middle class was developing. The "calling" to work justified a working class. The division of people into classes and occupations was, for Luther, the result of Divine Will. It is man's duty to persevere in his assigned place, he taught. Protestantism supported another aspect of the new economic system by discouraging wasteful consumption and the enjoyment of possessions. Calvin's concept of "maximum effort" laid a spiritual foundation for amassing capital. This powerful religious movement thus generated a high-production, high-investment mentality. It made self-denial in production and consumption both ethically right and economically effective.

Self-Destructing Ethic

Two centuries after the thinking of Luther and Calvin had begun working their effect on society, John Wesley (1703–1791) foresaw the likely negative outcome of such expressions of faith. Religion, he said, will produce industry and frugality which will lead to riches; as riches increase, so will pride, anger, and desire. Religion thus brings on its own decay.[6] It would be futile to try to prevent people from working and accumulating wealth, Wesley realized. His practical solution was to encourage them to do so and then to share their wealth so they would grow in grace.

Later, in young America, riches did indeed increase. Work and wealth became signs of respectability—a principal motivating force in people's lives. Religious forces drew people's attention to the secular life, but, in time, many lost sight of the treasures in heaven. Attempts to make the church of the saved visible in this world shifted people's concern from the hereafter to the here and now. Material success became an end in itself.

While Protestantism served early America well and laid the foundation for industrialization with its justification of work and investment, the industrial system eventually abused and then lost touch with that ethic. The notion of work as a spiritual calling fell out of sync with the mechanized work of mass production. The objective of work centered on economic gain, and even that was beyond the reach of many people. Industrialization eventually eroded the certainty that work would bring success to the individual. Semiskilled workers, trapped in the mills of the nineteenth century, realized that no amount of hard work would lift them to wealth or self-improvement.[7] Thus came the mounting negative feelings toward work and demands for more and more economic compensation in exchange for surrendering to such meaningless activity.

Work was no longer done for God's glorification; it took on a more utilitarian meaning. Ironically, what had been the foundation for industrialization was eventually eroded by it. American industry progressed, from that point, not on the work ethic but despite it. The Protestant ethic had taught people to work hard, save their money, and get their rewards in the future or the hereafter. But that message became perverted to a consumption ethic: "Work as little as possible, spend your money because it's shrinking in value, and demand your rewards now." By the 1960s, this trend culminated in the "me generation"—people devoted to self-gratification. The me-generation mentality affected more than just the youth of this country. Their parents had led the way in the scramble for houses, cars, appliances, and leisure-time goods; the youth merely expected more and then turned to new experiences when goods no longer satisfied their hunger.

Mixed Messages

The American brand of capitalism succeeded in creating such widespread prosperity relative to anything the world had ever seen that the imperative came to be one of consumption, not production. Demand for goods and services became the flywheel that kept the economic engine running fast and smooth. The spiritual dimension, meanwhile, faded as a justification for the accumulation of wealth. Whereas the Protestant view of work and wealth was once clear and present, it is now mixed at best. The individual seeking guidance in the Bible regarding those messages encounters some popular passages that admonish him to work and others that suggest that work is unimportant. For example, most Americans with any exposure to the New Testament will have heard Matt. 6:26—"Look at the birds of the air; they neither sow nor reap nor gather into barns, and yet your heavenly Father feeds them." The message seems to be: don't worry about working or storing up wealth. On the other hand, they may hear 2 Thess. 3:11–12—". . . we hear that some of you are living in idleness, mere busybodies, not doing any work. Now such persons we command and exhort in the Lord Jesus Christ to do their work in quietness and to earn their own living." And there is 1 Tim. 1:4—"If any would not work, neither should he eat."

Few verses are more widely known that those regarding the curse of wealth such as Matt. 19:23–24—". . . it will be very hard for rich people to enter the kingdom of heaven. Again I tell you, it is easier for a camel to go through the eye of a needle than for a rich man to enter the kingdom of God." Yet people may be led in the other direction by Matt. 25:29—"For to every person who has something, even more will be given, and he will have more than enough; but the person who has nothing, even the little that he has will be taken away from him."

Literal interpretations of selected passages from the New Testament do not necessarily convey the central message of Christianity. When people attempt to set guidelines for living and working in such a manner, they do not all arrive at the same conclusions. As a result, even those who are listening to "The Word" do not necessarily share a common ethic. In addition, biblical stories regarding wealth and poverty or servant and master seem hardly relevant to a society in which wealth is widespread and servant–master relationships have long since disappeared.

As John Wesley had feared, the Protestant ethic came to support an economic system that led to its own undoing. Today, our economic system is in danger of failing because it has no spiritual foundation despite the fact that many Americans assume a spiritual ethic is built into their political–economic system. After all, they believe, the United States is essentially a Christian nation.

A Christian Nation?

The nation's founders provided a philosophical base but not a religious one—especially not a specifically Christian one. Our founding fathers were influenced by Enlightenment thinking which matured in the eighteenth and nineteenth centuries. They believed that that all men were created equal and that, given the proper material and social conditions, fully realized human beings would evolve. If our institutions would conform to "natural law," man would develop his natural perfection, according to this utopian line of thought.

Enlightenment thinking also meshed well with the rise of science. By the eighteenth century, man's view of nature was changing in the Western world. Nature was no longer mysterious and divine. It had been reduced to a scientific machine, and man's place was to master this machine to produce wealth. America's seemingly unbounded resources and new frontiers promised material gain and freedom for man to fully realize his potential far beyond what some of the earlier Enlightenment thinkers may ever have dreamed. Economic expansion became part of America's destiny.

The Declaration of Independence, signed a century and a half after the white man began to settle the land, is a most humanitarian document, but it is not a Christian document. Thomas Jefferson, Benjamin Franklin, and George Washington rank among the greatest statesmen of all time, but they were deists out of the Enlightenment fashion, allowing that a supreme power had created the world but was no longer acting in its unfolding. The great document that launched America toward nationhood contains only three references to a divine being:

1. "equal station to which the Laws of Nature and of Nature's God entitle them"
2. "that they are endowed by their Creator"
3. "with a firm reliance on the protection of Divine Providence"

In its single reference to spiritual matters, our other great document, The Constitution, reads: "Congress shall make no law respecting an establishment of religion, or prohibiting the free exercise thereof." The reference was not made in the original articles, but added in the First Amendment! This nation, which so many citizens regarded as having built-in Christian values, was launched officially according to deist concepts but made no official recognition of a particular religion. We were given the foundation for a liberal society.

In time, the Protestant's concern for salvation gave way to the liberal's notion that society is perfectible. As man learned to read some of nature's laws, there seemed to be less need for divine intervention. Even Christians suspected that the Kingdom was coming on earth, that it was happening right here, and that one could be concerned with self-pursuits because "the system" would take care of thy neighbor. Moralists like Ben Franklin spoke of work and wealth in terms of usefulness rather than the glory of God.[8] Protestantism had begun to elevate the concept of wealth, and the pragmatism that developed in America raised it still higher. The old Protestant ethic was being secularized.

Rigid Rules

Eighteenth- and nineteenth-century America did have a strong Christian thrust despite the lack of official direction. The churches that took root in this land of freedom did not allow man to follow nature's laws, despite the intentions of the founding fathers. Quite the contrary! The early Protestants were no longer subject to the rule of the priests, but they lived under strict rules for daily conduct. Protestantism allowed everyone to be part of the "elect," but it enforced rigid rules for involvement in the secular world.

Early American churches left little room for the individual to fall victim to his wicked natural inclinations. "The core of Puritanism . . . was an intense moral zeal for the regulation of everyday conduct," says Daniel Bell. "Given the external dangers and psychological strains of living in a closed world, the individual had to be concerned not only with his own behavior but with the community."[9] Spiritual values were central to people's lives and tied all the elements of life into a meaningful whole.

Despite the tight religious rules for social conduct, preoccupation with individual salvation sometimes justified a person's acquisitiveness at the expense of others rather than as a blessing to be shared with others. Thus there was a religious "justification" for the inhumanities of the early days of the Industrial Revolution. Max Weber discussed the development of a bourgeois ethic which permitted the businessman to pursue his financial interests, enjoy a supply of industrious workers, and assure himself that unequal economic distribution was the result of Divine Providence.[10] By the twentieth century, increased prosperity and the attainment of greater economic and social equality had undermined the notion of high calling for both businessman and laborer. Even at the beginning of this century, Weber was able to note that the idea of duty in one's calling "prowls about in our lives like the ghost of dead religious beliefs."[11]

Protestantism has carried within itself a fundamental conflict between individualism and community. When economic interests conflict with the central Christian message of love and sharing, some

Protestants divorce their private life and their religion from their public activities. They focus on individual religious experiences.[12] For some, this leads to concern for grace and being one of the "elect" and generates hostility rather than compassion for sinners. Martin Marty, in *Righteous Empire*, describes the division between personal and community concern. "Private" Protestantism, beginning especially in the early nineteenth century, stressed individual salvation and the moral life of the "saved." Its followers were concerned with conversion and reaffirmation of faith. They were out to save souls. "Public" Protestantism, on the other hand, was more concerned with social order and man's social role. Adherents worked for transformation of the world; they were out to save society.[13]

In recent years, religion has become an internalized, private affair for many Americans. Following the peak of public party Protestantism in the 1960s, with its highly visible mobilization for civil rights and against war, the private side has returned to the fore. Perhaps, with the rise of big systems—government, business, and labor unions—the individual has seen little choice but to retreat inward.

The interplay of religion, social development, and economic growth over American history is much too complex to treat fully here. Cause and effect are not easily distinguished and invite oversimplification. We can safely conclude, however, that the underlying spiritual dimension to work and the predominant view of man have changed significantly over the past two centuries. As people turn inward, many find their work has no meaning. Although some embrace the more traditional, self-denial values that provide meaning for their work, far more find the contrast between what they believe they are and what the workplace expects of them too great to bear. They may rebel at the pressures that threaten to compress or extinguish their spirituality. The workplace is one of the principal places where they strike out against their loss of power and the fragmentation of their lives. The old Protestant ethic taught people to deny their selfish desires and work for greater social and spiritual glory, but denying oneself does not seem to make sense in an era of rational and scientific thinking. Many, including a significant portion of those in the ranks of traditional religions, embrace the humanist notion that man's highest goal is progress here on earth. Their concerns, whether personal or societal, are essentially secular.

Many of us stand naked with neither spiritual connection nor social agreement to give purpose to our work. In the late nineteenth century, we had regarded ourselves as the chosen nation. Less than a century later, the country which had fought World War II convinced that God was on its side waged a nonwar in Vietnam that it hoped God wouldn't hear about. Blood-letting in the ghettos and on the campuses revealed our inner conflicts and suggested that we were hypocrites who could no longer hide our selfish, inhumane, un-Christian tendencies. Scarcities and uncertainties have risen up to dampen our traditional eagerness to meet the future. Rather than striking at the heart of the problem, we expect to do little more than cope with an undesirable situation. We have given up the notion of the perfectibility of man. We try instead to fine-tune our institutions to compensate for our individual shortcomings. Our institutions are of less and less help in the struggle, however, because they were designed to serve an ethic of consumption rather than the earlier calling to work that opposed immediate gratification of desires. The early success of capitalism had been built, not on the "impulse to acquisition," but on the restraint of that impulse.[14] But that discipline of worker and businessman has been lost.

While the old Protestant ethic or some vestige of it is still at work in some people's lives, it is not the predominant influence on attitudes toward work today. After centuries of its undoing there is little reason to expect a return to widespread acceptance of the old ethic. We should, instead, look to see if there is a new work ethic that can be articulated for our time. We should look, too, at why our organizations are failing to bring together the work that needs to be done and the needs that people could satisfy through work.

4

What Went Wrong at Work?

A FACTORY WORKER FINDS EXCUSES to abandon his work station, a sales clerk makes us feel we are intruding on his reverie when we hand him our selection, an industrial salesman consistently works a four-hour day, and a city building inspector fakes his reports. Not everyone, but perhaps a substantial minority of Americans, is performing poorly at work or avoiding work altogether.

Why, when millions of people want jobs so badly, do so many people perform so badly in their jobs?

If work has the potential for filling so many of our needs, why do so many people derive so little satisfaction from their work?

Those of us who are victims in one way or another—as customers, managers, or fellow workers—are overwhelmed by "evidence" that the old work ethic is dead. We blame the worker and assume the organization is faultless. Yet, I have heard many workers complain that they cannot contribute enough on the job. They are frustrated because no one listens to their ideas, they don't get treated with enough respect, or the boss isn't concerned about quality—only with getting the product out the door. They complain that the other guy doesn't work hard enough—that others lack the will to work.

Survey after survey, however, indicates that most people really do want to work. In fact, studies by the Public Agenda Foundation show that workers often give more to their jobs than their bosses expect of them and yet are giving less to the job than they could. In one

37

of its surveys, only 22 percent of the workers said they were performing to their full capacity.[1] The other 78 percent, then, leaves plenty of room for improvement. For that matter, even those who feel they are working at full capacity may not really be doing so.

In another study, done for the U.S. Chamber of Commerce, nearly nine out of ten workers said that it is personally important to them to work hard and do their best.[2] This is supported by the three out of four workers, in a Connecticut Mutual Life Insurance Co. study, who said they frequently feel a sense of dedication to their work.[3] The desire and the capacity to do better are there, but for some reason they aren't being converted into good work behavior.

One thing is for certain, regardless of the quality of work performed: more and more people are working or seeking work. In the last thirty years, America has created 40 million new jobs as it kept pace not only with a growing population but with a growing percentage of that population that wanted to work. In 1980, 63 percent of the population age sixteen or over was participating in the labor force. This compares with 59 percent a quarter-century earlier.

Even a greater percentage of the youth of this country have come to work while continuing their education. Although children are no longer employed on millions of family farms as they once were, we do see them working at the local fast-food restaurants, gas stations, and department stores. Enterprising children in Manhattan wash windshields for a quarter as cars stop for traffic lights. Suburban teenage boys canvass their communities with handbills advertising their housepainting services.

Something is attracting or driving more and more people to work. Work is meeting some, if not all, of their needs. In many cases, the moving force seems to be primarily or entirely financial; the work itself is merely the means to some other end. Yet, we should note that they *are* choosing work as the route to financial reward.

We may be troubled when we see people attain financial support without working. We may be bothered by the fact that some seemingly undeserving people are on the welfare rolls. It's true that the number of welfare programs and the number of benefit recipients have grown over recent decades as we have enacted legislation to extend a helping hand farther and farther. Once aimed at only those who were truly unable to work—the very young, the very old, and the handicapped—welfare programs have been broadened to give economic sustenance to able-bodied people as well. Yet, most people who are on the welfare rolls get off within a year.

People receiving welfare—even those who abuse the system—

should give us less cause to suspect the work ethic is dead than the millions more who are at work but performing badly. We may feel some economic and psychological drag because we support those who are not in the labor force, but we cannot blame the existence of welfare for the poor behavior of those who are employed. The individual performing below potential is not holding back because some small percentage of his or her earnings is channeled to people who aren't working. The problem lies in the individual's work relationship; the satisfaction derived either through the contribution made in the work itself or through the rewards obtained from the work situation is inadequate.

Growing Mismatch

The key reason for poor work behavior today is the extreme mismatch between what people want from work and what they can get from it. Most Americans are not dissatisfied with work per se, says Michael Maccoby in his book *The Leader.* "But, increasingly, they are dissatisfied and demoralized by the way work is organized and led. The work ethic is not dead, but it has not been articulated for this age."[4]

In a study for Sentry Insurance Company, 76 percent of the public sampled said most people have less pride in their work today than workers did ten years ago; 76 percent said employees are less loyal to their companies; 73 percent feel that the motivation to work is not as strong as it was; and 71 percent feel workmanship is worse than it was ten years ago.[5] This type of survey, however, reflects how people perceive the behavior of others—behavior, but not necessarily underlying wants. In the surveys mentioned earlier, people expressing their own inner values and their thoughts on what ought to be showed a high degree of interest in working effectively.

Failure to do a good job does not necessarily reflect the loss of a work ethic. The evidence suggests that something is getting in the way of the desire to work and causing negative behavior. Beneath disinterest, laziness, and anger may lie the desire to work, contribute, and participate. There is little doubt that there has been a decline in work behavior, but this does not mean the work ethic has deteriorated. The problem, say Daniel Yankelovich and John Immerwahr of the Public Agenda Foundation, is that our management systems and work incentives do not match today's workers.[6]

If the work ethic were dead, we would not only have to question why more and more Americans are participating in the workforce, but we would have to explain why so many people work so hard at their leisure-time pursuits. The United States has been called "the gene pool of the discontented." We have traditionally been a restless, ambitious nation. Americans charge enthusiastically into their non-work activities—hobbies, exercise, sports, and night or weekend school. Many are pushing for peak performance off the job. Despite the impression that Americans spend most of their free hours loung-ing in front of their television sets, they aren't loafing. They are engaged primarily in purposeful leisure-time pursuits, says Dr. John Pollock, president of Research and Forecasts Inc., a company that has done numerous surveys on values, work attitudes, and use of leisure time. I asked him, "You mean the work ethic isn't dead?" His answer: "It certainly isn't. We're the kind of people the Pilgrims would have wanted us to be!"

The work ethic may be stronger now than it has been for many years. Peter Drucker has pointed out that in the past hundred years, it was "progressive" to ease married women and older persons from the workforce. During those years, we were really trying to under-mine people's search for work, he says. In the last twenty years, however, we have seen the work ethic return with a "vengeance."[7]

High Hopes, Low Return

With so many reasons for working and so many people coming to work, what causes the disappointing behavior that leads us to assume that people don't want to work? What is getting in the way of what people would like to bring to work and take from it? Why have pride, workmanship, and loyalty to the company declined?

We might assume that people are coming to work primarily for the money and expecting little else. Yet, we see more people today than ever doing their best to prepare themselves to get a "good job." Many of the youth in college—and the adults there as well—are job-oriented. They want to acquire credentials for the best possible job. And that includes more than just "top pay." For them, the desire to work is not dead, and something besides money is attracting them.

Soon after these young people enter a job situation, however, they very quickly display what looks like the absence of a work ethic. They don't want to do what they're told to do. We have a tremendous mismatch between what people want to do and what the situation al-lows them to do when they go to work. Society encourages people to get an education, think for themselves, and to grow. Then, it expects them to be content in job situations where they are not allowed to grow or be enterprising or creative. As a result, we have a clash. The worker either turns off and demands only more and more pay or stays turned on and challenges his supervisors step by step.

It was quite natural to assume that when tough economic times returned—as they did in the early 1980s—the workforce would become more compliant. But that did not happen. The mismatch between what people wanted and what the work situation provided continued to cause problems of quality performance. The fact that they still came to work demanding to be treated as a valuable resource even in a weak job market should have been taken as evidence of a strong work ethic, not the absence of one.

Many people expect far more from work than what their predecessors did because they feel they bring more to it. They are driven to find something to which they can invest a greater portion of themselves. They do not find a reciprocal situation, however. Their expectations and, in many cases, their talents are higher and broader than the available jobs require. Because of this mismatch, people either avoid work because it meets too few of their needs, or come to work and demand that the system meet more of their needs than it traditionally has. Either way, the mismatch causes the quality and quantity of work to fall short of what we want and need. For many, the work situation—either the work itself or the organizational relationships—is deadening. The mismatch has been worsening because many jobs and organizations have changed very little while people have been changing a great deal.

Man has probably always struggled to adapt to the work at hand. Primal man undoubtedly had some adjustment problems fitting into a band of hunters. For the hunter–gatherer, which man has been for most of his history, simple farming must have demanded a painful adjustment. But each of these steps seems to be a natural progression upward toward greater realization of what it means to be human—to employ one's intelligence and social skills.

The routinized jobs created by industrialization over the last 200 years, however, reversed this process for the millions of people who have performed mindless tasks. Their adjustment has been downward. And the pain of that adjustment has been intensified by the fruits of industrialization. As people's standard of living rose and freedoms outside the job grew, the contrast with the situation at work was heightened. Today's workers are less and less willing to tolerate that gap. Refusal to surrender to the work situation may be the result of young workers valuing different things than their predecessors, older workers changing what they value, or older workers expressing wants that they have previously suppressed.[8]

Daniel Yankelovich and John Immerwahr point out that there has been a shift toward jobs where the individual worker has significant control over the quality and quantity of work for three reasons. First, service-industry workers are more likely to say they have freedom in how they do their jobs than are workers in manufacturing industries, and the service-industry jobs have been growing faster. The same is true for white-collar versus blue-collar workers. Second, new technology is giving workers more discretion. In their survey of American jobholders, Yankelovich and Immerwahr found that 44 percent had experienced significant technological change and of these 74 percent said their work had become less routine and more interesting. Third, there is more discretion in the workplace because of the nature of the people themselves. New people with new values are placing new demands on the employer, but this does not mean these values are incompatible with hard work.[9]

Many of today's jobs permit workers to exercise more discretion in carrying out their duties than do jobs linked closely to the pace of machines or production processes. An increasing percentage of our workforce—even in nonmanagement, nonprofessional ranks—is able to set its own pace, determine the details of carrying out its work, and even neglect certain details or modes of good behavior. At the same time, workers are often subjected to heavily controlled management systems. They may have to meet certain standards for attendance, completion of paperwork, sales or production, and other responsibilities. Yet, they may be able to do so without really attending to the quality of the product or service. While the systems may give management an illusion of control, the worker has latitude for falling short of a quality job from the point of view of the customer or the next person in the process. The more a job involves service, flexibility, and creativity, the less it is truly controllable.

People who seek high-discretion work may strongly identify with the modern work ethic and, therefore, not be responsive to traditional management techniques and incentives. This makes them highly volatile. They can become turned off when work fails to meet their needs, and they are in a position to do considerable damage to their area of the business.

Many people have run past the available jobs in terms of education, experience, and expectations. Some managers believe that perhaps the people are right and the jobs are wrong. The problem may not be the people but what they have encountered in job content and organizational structures and procedures. We may fail to see the underlying work ethic because it manifests itself in ways that do not fit our expectations since we are looking at the situation from the system's point of view.

American Telephone and Telegraph reversed its view in the early 1960s. Its employee attitude surveys were suggesting that the people were okay but the work wasn't, recalls one AT&T executive. That led the company to venture into "job enrichment" efforts and, later, into quality-of-worklife concepts to capitalize on people's inherent motivation to work and to provide more fulfilling job situations for them.

Overqualified and Unsuited

Suddenly, we seem to have a more highly educated workforce than we can employ. Until recently, Americans believed that the job market could always absorb people with more and more education. In fact, one of the chief purposes of our educational efforts has been to prepare people for work. Education to stimulate and satisfy the quest for knowledge and for the development of human potential, on the other hand, has too often been only a minor consideration. Although people have been exposed to an increasing amount of schooling, the educational sector has not been doing an especially good job of building either an appreciation for one's own potential for development or positive attitudes toward work. The schools have become more concerned about supplying "credentials" for work.

Generations ago, workers denied their own aspirations and settled for economic subsistence; they worked for the family, and they looked for the day when their children could get something more out of life than they did. What began as a desire to help the children find less degrading work and better-paying jobs eventually became perverted into a drive to get the children to qualify for positions that would involve as little work as possible. By the 1960s, parents were pushing their children into universities to prepare for they knew not what. The message was one of avoidance; it did not encourage a quest for knowledge and growth. Thanks to overeager parents and much-too-accommodating educators, the children generally were inspired neither to enjoy the subject matter to which they were being exposed nor to prepare for some specific, meaningful job. Thus, we had thousands of turned-off youth, a generation gap, and job mismatches.

In the early post–World War II years, youth were taught to avoid work, to get an "education," get a "soft" job, go into the military services and retire in twenty years, or otherwise get all they could from the beneficent system. Young workers looked for pensions, fringe benefits, and security. By the 1960s, the young were seeking anything but jobs in the system. In the 1970s, the next wave of youth came back to the system, expecting big money, challenge, humanistic treatment, self-fulfillment, and a chance to help society. They wanted to be big consumers and substantial producers. They wanted it all. They got very little. By the thousands, college graduates searched unsuccessfully for challenging work. The job hunt wore many of them down, and they settled for jobs as secretaries, waitresses, bartenders, and cab drivers. Time and again, they had heard the line: "Sorry, you're overqualified." With their credentials, employers feared, these eager young people would quickly become bored. College graduates couldn't plug into the system in ways that were meaningful to them, and some had doubts about whether they should even try to plug in. Although they were trying hard to make a start on their career paths, many of them knew they would not find it easy to make the sacrifices the system would demand of them.

The problem of being overqualified or, at least, perceiving oneself as overqualified has been building for decades. For many years, employers have contributed to the problem. They first used high school diplomas and then college degrees to sort out the most promising workers even when the specific job required much less educational attainment. Since diplomas and degrees may reflect intelligence, attainment, and some willingness to play by the rules, they became the mandatory passports to employment.

When educational requirements exceed the actual needs of the job they lead to a bumping-back process. An overqualified person takes a certain job and the person with lesser credentials is bumped back to a lesser job. As a result, more and more people wind up in jobs for which they are indeed overqualified. The values that would have led people to do good work serve only to sensitize them to their mismatch and invite poor work behavior.

Although the value of the many years of schooling that some people acquire can be debated, those who have the diplomas and degrees are convinced that they have some special assets to bring to the job and, perhaps, some special rights to rewarding work since they played by the rules that used to provide an edge in getting what one wanted in the job market. We may deride youth for their high expectations, for wanting to "use their education," or for being unrealistic in their feelings of entitlement, but the fact is that they are set on personal growth. We have fueled their interest in work and then thwarted it.

Systematic Suppression

As we observe people's work behavior, we don't always see the underlying forces behind their actions. Take, for example, the department store clerk who is working after school to earn college funds. It seems that whenever the customer lines are longest at her cash register, someone presents a personal check. The clerk is not allowed to approve the check, however. She is looking at the customer. She can inspect his proof of identity. But company rules say she must go to a supervisor who has the "authority" to approve acceptance of the check. That supervisor may be a sixteenth of a mile across the store, but she has the red pen with which to indicate official approval. Without seeing the customer or his identification, the supervisor places her initials on the check, thereby permitting business to resume.

The clerk returns to her cash register to find the line longer and the customers angrier. She is caught in the middle—between the rules of the system and the need to serve the customers who are confronting her. She is not able to use her discretion in doing the basic job of serving the customer. As she sees people becoming dissatisfied and, sometimes, downright hostile, she may well feel the situation reflects on her competence. She may, then, use her thwarted discretion to avoid work and abuse the customer by hiding in the backroom, working slowly, or acting discourteously.

A worker's behavior reflects not only the systems and rules but the emphasis coming from management through stated or implied directions. If the sales clerk attends to that electronic cash register and abuses you, remember that in her two-day training period upon being hired she may have been taught how to operate the cash register but not how to serve the customer. When she was assigned to this particular department, no one may have told her where various items are displayed or explained to her the features of the products. It's possible that no one she has met in the company has demonstrated concern that she serve the customer well. The basic message she has received is likely to have been simply: "Be there." Why, then, should she take it upon herself to learn what's what and what's where? Confronting customers can be an ordeal for the young and unskilled. It is far more comfortable to stand away from the action and talk with fellow clerks or chat on the telephone.

Many young people do not have adequate models or educational preparation to reinforce their work ethic and convert it into positive behavior. Some do not have the self-discipline and drive for personal growth that family and school should have nurtured but didn't. They suffer not from an inherent human fault but from the failings of the culture in which they have grown up.

Many jobs, established on the assumption that workers will have poor attitudes and not perform well on their own, actually nurture negative behavior. Some employers build in the expectation of high turnover and provide little, if any, training. In the Gallup study for the United States Chamber of Commerce, nine out of ten workers said it is personally important to them to work hard on their jobs and do their best. Nearly half of them said they are "very concerned" about providing top quality product and services, and another 37 percent said they are "somewhat concerned."[10] Yet, 55 percent of these workers indicated they had received no on-the-job training in the past year, and 65 percent had had no off-the-job training.

Controls and systems, rather than training, are the popular means of shaping behavior in business organizations. Because they are simpler to understand than people, they appeal to managers as shortcuts to improve productivity and quality. Workers, including managers, can make mistakes. That's why companies build systems of controls to catch errors. When they rely more on controls than discretion and judgment, however, they may lower the quality of product and service, infuriate customers, and frustrate employees.

Chatting with a grocery store manager at a party one night, I asked him about check-cashing procedures in his store. He quickly admitted that it was a problem that frustrated both customers and clerks. "All procedure is the reaction to error," he explained. "To prevent an error, we go through a procedure thousands of times—over and over again. We do it despite the fact that doing so may cause even more errors and much greater inefficiencies."

If people have a negative view of these control systems, it seems only fair. Company procedures, controls, and policies are—after all—based largely on a negative view of people. They box people in so that the misfits will be kept in check, so that the dishonest cannot take unfair advantage, so that the indolent will be where they ought to be. As a result, many organizations are run at the pace of the slowest and least capable or dependable.

When companies let controls run the business, they block creativity and commitment. If employees are intimidated rather than helped to do their fundamental jobs by procedures and paperwork, they may lose any sense of dedication and involvement they had. The organization that establishes too many rules may nurture a corps of "just because" managers—people who enforce rules simply because they exist. This type of manager becomes more concerned about the worker's being there than what he or she actually does and what is preventing the worker from doing a good job.

The just-because attitude intensifies two naturally occurring problems in organizations: specialization, and managerial fear and ignorance. Some specialization or departmentalization is necessary in most organizations, but it becomes a deterrent to effective work when people fail to see the bigger picture beyond their own particular area of responsibility. Departmentalization can lead to people's getting the impression that they are isolated, that they don't relate to what others in the organization are doing. If I am far down in the hierarchy, it's all too likely that I don't know what the corporation is out to do, how it is doing, or what I can do to help. The situation seems to be "me versus the company" if I want to meet my quotas, stay within my budget, and get a pay raise. Any interest I have in developing my talents, suggesting new ideas, or improving organizational effectiveness doesn't fit into the budget or relate to the factors on which I am being evaluated, so I do only what's required. To the outsider, therefore, it may look like I have no initiative—no work ethic.

We sometimes forget that God didn't create departments. Man created departments and specialization to make effective organizations. Too much attention to procedures may obscure the big picture and distract people from the detail of the work they should be doing. The details with which they become concerned are those of procedure, not the details of the fundamental job.

The just-because syndrome also feeds the natural fear and ignorance that exists in an organization. Throughout the ranks of management we can find people who are intimidated by their role and ignorant of many of the things they need to know. In light of the demands placed upon managers, some measure of fear and ignorance is quite natural and forgivable. The more the system makes them fear making a mistake, the more intense their awareness of the things they don't know. Still, this situation makes them less likely to adapt and learn. They give orders. They are afraid to take the time to listen to employees. They can't risk doing something new. Ignorance of all the facts is a constant human situation, but hiding behind the rules and saying "just because" undermines both the manager and his or her subordinates in any attempt to work at full potential.

Not all rules and limitations have been concocted by management, however. Workers, especially through their labor unions, have fought hard to preserve low-discretion, narrowly defined jobs. This has tended to preserve the status quo in jobs while people have been changing, thereby widening the gap between what people want and what they can get.

The workplace is so bound in rules that it is often difficult to tell whether a particular rule was originated by management or union, or whether it was dreamed up by an individual employee on the spur of the moment. For example, a seventy-six-year-old woman was told by her twenty-six-year-old telephone installer that he couldn't put the new phone where she wanted it because he would have to move her desk. He was not allowed to move furniture, he said. Whether he was bound by such a rule or simply made it up to match other workrules he had learned, he had an alibi. So the woman said, "Here, I'll show you how to move a desk." and proceeded to shove it out of the way for him. She had little sympathy for a person who measures his "success" or status in terms of how limited his job is—who so willingly hides behind "rules."

The Packaging of Work

Most of us, in our capacities as worker, manager, parent, or educator, as well as the economists and politicians, have done great harm to the concept of work. We have "packaged" it to be sold or rented by the hour. We have stripped it of close association with a product or service. Work has come to mean "job"—a commodity. And, as such, it has become separated from its deeper human connections.

Good work or success has come to be equated with promotion and status. In many ways, even minor clues indicate that status is more important than doing the job well. An executive secretary (the title is a bit of status in itself) who types ten letters a week may get the newest, most sophisticated typewriter. It comes with the drapes and carpeting. The newly hired typist whose job it is to type all day long, however, gets the rebuilt clunker that requires monthly repairs. Her hope is to be promoted to a position where she will get better equipment for which she will have little use.

Upbringing, models, education, and work experiences often send out messages that work is a commodity and not a particularly desirable one. It's little wonder, then, that it looks like too few people are being driven by a work ethic. However, if the surveys are close to accurate, we are not a nation of people who don't want to work. We do not face the impossible task of changing human nature. We must, instead, capitalize on human nature by first changing some of our assumptions about people and, then, altering our job structures so that work can be both economically effective and personally rewarding.

We cannot move backwards, taking away freedom, mobility, or education. And few of us would want to return to the "good old days" when people would submit to any controls imposed on them. People used to work seventy and eighty hours a week to feed the family. Do we want that again? Would that be the best evidence of a work ethic?

The self-denial approach to work would not be suited to the jobs of the future. The highly schooled, high aspiring people coming into the workplace are better prepared for the high-technology society that lies ahead than for today's workplace. But we complain that their aspirations are too high, they want to do things differently, they want to have too much "say" in things. They are interested and active individuals ready for the jobs of the future, yet we try to harness them with the jobs, incentives, and controls of the past.

Negative Synergy

Over the past couple of decades, American management has concentrated on priorities other than the quality of product or service. Old-time companies and long-trusted products have been absorbed and then lost in larger corporations. In time, many of them have become the victims of cost-reduction and corner-cutting, resulting in the erosion of both customer loyalties and employee loyalties.

When we buy a product that doesn't work properly or experience a breakdown in a relatively new one, we complain about poor workmanship. But it is not the bottom-rung workers who are to blame in all cases. I have cussed many times when a hair dryer, lawn mower, or vacuum cleaner has failed well before I think its time is up. What is even worse, in many cases, is the fact that the device is not repairable. Designed with low-cost materials and intended for low-cost production methods, parts are snap fit, friction fit, or put together with adhesives in ways that do not lend themselves to being taken apart—to say nothing of being put back together again.

Generally, these products are assembled just as they were supposed to be. They do not represent sloppy workmanship on the part of the people making the parts or putting them together. But some-one—engineers and managers—may have specified materials, designs, and production methods that don't result in durable, repairable products.

I have asked so many employees in manufacturing plants what bothers them most about their work that I now challenge others to do the same and tell me if they do not find that 90 percent of the complaints will have to do with the condition of the equipment, the quality of materials, the work flow, or procedures that prevent workers from turning out products they can be proud of. People know what dependable products are when they buy them, and they are just as perceptive when they are producing them. When a machinist sees that one out of four parts he turns out goes into the scrap bin because the workpieces are below standard or his machine is not functioning properly, he can't help wondering why management doesn't care about quality. The worker who can't respect his product or his supervisor has two strikes against his exerting maximum effort. Management has to make it known that quality is a high priority—not simply by saying so, but by listening to worker's complaints and suggestions and following up with action.

While the focus of management attention on mergers and growth through acquisition of other companies has undermined quality and loyalty in many cases, some top executives justify their merger game-playing as a means of pooling financial power, marketing strength, or technological capabilities to form stronger companies. Theoretically, a good merger will have some synergistic effects so that the new organization will be even greater than the sum of its parts. Two and two will equal, not four, but five. Unfortunately, many mergers have worked a *negative synergy*. The dealmakers may come out ahead, but the average shareholder, the employees, and the customers don't always fare as well as they did before the merger.

The increased contact and interchange among people in a growing organization should result in synergistic effects. In many mergers, however, larger structures and ax-wielding tend to work against the feelings of being "a company" or community. People either lose their jobs or work under a cloud of possible dismissal. Cooperation among strangers never quite gets into gear, and, as corporate machinery becomes more complex, even old friendships wither. What looks good on paper doesn't seem to work out in the real world.

An old-faithful secretary with decades of service has been moved to a new department in her recently merged company. Seated amidst strangers and no longer in contact with friends in other departments, she feels lost and useless. She laments to me, a visitor: "I sure miss the days when we were a *company*." I think, "That's too bad for her." Then I realize that the company has suffered a loss, too. Numerous inefficiencies and slippages in quality of service provided internally and to outsiders have developed because management has failed to use this woman's storehouse of information and contacts throughout other departments—a resource that had once contributed to a smooth-running operation.

Intangibles such as worker loyalty and willingness to take the extra steps to produce quality contribute to a company's favorable financial performance. Their loss causes a decline in the product and profit for the merged company that management can't explain. Valuable, informal lines of communication become ineffective as people are shifted around or dropped from the payroll. Formal procedures, no matter how sophisticated or expensive, don't make effective substitutes.

Large institutions have a tendency to become highly depersonalized. System and procedure may so oppose individual effort that workers become uncooperative with management and with one another. Workers fight the system and fellow workers as their work-lives become a scream for recognition and significance. People must prove to themselves as well as to others that they exist; to do so, some may choose to immobilize their machines, refuse service to a customer, or foul up the paperwork—negative synergies that management didn't count on! The person trying, nevertheless, to do a good job may find requisitioning supplies such an ordeal in triplicate that it seems justifiable to double or triple-order, steal what's needed, or to skip the work for which the supplies are needed. More negative synergies!

A Sense of Worth

The challenge to improve quality seems to pose a choice between reverting to smaller business entities or personalizing and humanizing the larger organizations. But that's no choice at all because even a small business can be impersonal. Therefore, the only option is to personalize and humanize all our business entities, large and small, to allow people to feel a sense of worth.

Loss of economic opportunity threatens everyone, but it is not so great a threat to a work ethic as people's being treated only in economic terms. People need to know they make a difference. Their sense of self-worth depends not only upon being employed but upon the manner in which they are introduced to the job, trained, and even the way they can expect to be dismissed from a job. They need recognition for work well done and simply for being a person.

One corporate manager with many years' experience with his company became a victim of a recent merger. One morning, as he arrived at the office, his new boss told him: "Today's your last day. Clean out your office and be gone in thirty minutes. And I'd appreciate it if you wouldn't speak to anyone about this on the way out." A young secretary in another company found herself part of an organizational shake-up. Late one afternoon she was told this had been her last day. "Clear off your desk and pick up your paycheck," she was told. In an instant, these persons' relationships with fellow workers were severed. Their opportunity to be part of an organization in which they could grow and learn was ended abruptly. The veteran concluded that all he had contributed meant nothing to the company. The young woman learned early in her career that there's no guarantee that one's loyalty will be reciprocated.

Management can't guarantee people perpetual employment, but it does need to make people feel confident that they will be treated fairly and humanely. Although few people will commit blindly to a job today, many have the potential for a far more meaningful and productive commitment than was possible in the past. Whether this commitment is made depends on the quality of leadership they encounter in the organization.

Two midwestern companies were suffering the pains of overdiversification and weakness in traditional product lines in the late 1970s. At one of them, the chief executive officer not only pruned away dozens of high-ranking managers, he let it be known that if you had been with the company three years and hadn't risen several levels, you couldn't be very valuable. By contrast, when John J. Nevin became chairman of troubled Firestone Tire & Rubber Company in 1980, he headed a major purge of facilities and inventories. Although he made changes in the executive ranks, he did most of his recruiting inside Firestone. His new president, Lee Brodeur, was a thirty-year veteran of the company.

Character Shift

A new American social character is taking shape, says Michael Maccoby. This character has three potentially negative traits: alienation, self-indulgent consumer orientation, and rebelliousness. No work ethic would be possible if these traits prevail; in fact, no social ethic or ideals would be possible, he says.[11]

"The key to developing the American character is the workplace," Maccoby believes.[12] He sees it as the potential means of turning character toward its positive side because that's where so much depression begins. Many managers would not agree that people's negative attitudes are formed at work, however; such managers are frequently frustrated, in fact, because they feel they are expected to battle the negative feelings and depression that people bring to work—the results of personal and family problems and social conditions.

We could debate endlessly whether American depression begins in the workplace or outside it because it has countless sources. The important question to deal with is where to begin attacking the depression. Because the workplace can offer rich resources for building people through leadership, training, and work experience that tests technical and social skills, it has the potential for being a positive force in people's lives. We must look beyond ways to rid the factory and office of dissatisfaction and find ways to generate positive feelings and satisfaction. If people can be permitted to find a sense of meaning and nurture some life skills on the job, they will be better equipped to deal with problems originating both on and off the job.

We can neither define nor solve the problems of poor work performance and the inadequate satisfaction derived from work when we segment the source of trouble according to job or nonjob origin, when we segment the values we bring to work from those we take home, or when we segment work from the rest of our lives. We must find leaders who can help us integrate rather than segment our lives.

With the proper leadership, says Michael Maccoby, negative traits could be converted to positive ones. Although Americans are essentially egoistic today, the individual need not wallow in narcissism and disregard the rest of society. Maccoby believes people could become more experimental and tolerant (rather than alienated), more interested in self-development (rather than merely indulging in consumption), and more participative (rather than rebellious).[13] In fact, these qualities could become the basis for a brand new ethic—one of self-development, says Maccoby. The workplace can be the vehicle for nurturing this ethic and for enabling people to respond to it.

Asserting that the work ethic is dead is a superficial and misleading way of referring to a more complex situation. It diverts our attention from those things that could unlock people's many reasons for working and performing well. It engenders negative feelings about people rather than lets us turn to structuring and packaging work so that it invites better job behavior.

Today, our organizational structures and management systems tend to lock out the work ethic. Unfortunately, those who take the soft approach to correcting the mismatch of jobs and people generally strive to lessen people's unhappiness by seeking ways to enable them to escape work rather than by helping them find satisfaction of their many needs through work. Those who take the harder approach would rip up the work ethic, with its roots running deep into our culture, and transplant it in the shallow soil of rules and procedures.

5

End of the Consumption Binge

A UNITED AIRLINES STEWARDESS EXPLAINS TO A PASSENGER that although she has ten years' seniority, she has lost her first choice of routes because of cutbacks in employment. "I'm not used to going backwards, but a lot of other people are going *nowhere*. I'm thankful for having a job. I never thought, ten years ago, that by this time I would be thankful just for that."

On a subzero night in January 1983, 20,000 people began lining up to apply for 200 job openings at A. O. Smith Corporation in Milwaukee. Most of them realized they were going nowhere. Nevertheless, they were trying to keep up.

Many Americans have a feeling of going backwards. For many, real take-home pay has shrunk. The average production worker's weekly earnings—adjusted for inflation—peaked in 1972 at $198 and then fell to $168 by 1982. In the quarter-century ending in 1972, American workers had experienced gains in weekly earnings in twenty-two years and decreases in only three. Their fortunes changed dramatically in the decade after that when decreases outnumbered increases seven to three.

The recessions of 1980–1983 were more than cyclical downturns; they were the harbingers of an age that will be different from the three postwar decades in which economic growth seemed automatic. The mighty productive engine of America had somehow turned into a giant consumption machine that was running out of wherewithal for buying the goods that signified success. People looked at the hard realities and lowered their expectations for the future—their own and that of their children.

The millions of people who left the farms and came to the factories earlier in this century were responding to a consumption ethic, not a work ethic. They found the work attractive only because it provided the economic basics and a chance to improve their standard of living. They did well. They became part of the richest nation in the world. They went on a consumption binge that far exceeded their survival and safety needs as they tried, also, to meet their needs for love and esteem through consumption. They sought recognition and admiration from others for the goods they acquired or the experiences they consumed in vacations, weekend activities, or after-hours pursuits.

Much of this consumption was a cover-up for depression caused by the lack of real personal growth and inadequate satisfaction of higher needs. The consumption era that we have just been through since World War II was simply a "happy pill" to mask our depression, Fred Herzberg has told me several times. He is deeply concerned that too many people suffer the lack of character development and, therefore, search unsuccessfully for something to fill the emptiness in their lives.

We have fallen victim to a psychology of affluence, claims Daniel Yankelovich. The symptoms of this affliction include: (1) an "ampersand mentality" (we want a high standard of living in both material and nonmaterial dimensions); (2) the tendency to regard expectations as entitlements; (3) taking it for granted that the economy will function well automatically; and (4) turning self-denial on its head in exchange for duty to self.[1]

Because we have been so caught up in the present and unwilling to put off gratification, we have lost the orientation to the future in which so many generations before us found excitement. Now we can see around us the signs of a society that concerns itself with immediate gratification and neglects the long term. Our infrastructure is run down, the Social Security system may not furnish security much longer, massive federal deficits defy control, and a frightening number of businesses lack the capital to invest in the future.

Escapism reduced our value as producers as we became distracted by all the good things to consume. In the years since World War II, we have become masters of mass selling, mass advertising, and mass credit facilities to stimulate consumption. One federal administration after another has stimulated demand to keep the economy rolling and provide employment for a nation that seemed to be losing interest in working. The old Protestant ethic has been stood on its head in our tax structures. Americans are taxed on the interest and dividends earned in savings accounts or other forms of investment that would purchase the tools of production. On the other hand, those who borrow money to buy a car, an appliance, or a vacation are permitted to deduct the interest they pay from their income taxes. We have built into the system countless biases that favor consumption over production.

For over thirty years, the growth ethic has predominated. People have watched to see how much company sales grew, how much gross national product grew, or how much corporate and personal earnings grew. With an economy fueled by World War II, the Cold War, the Korean War, and the Vietnam War, Americans responded to challenges from the ghetto far out into the galaxy while lavishing goods and services upon themselves. They placed heavy demands on the economic system through personal consumption and public programs but were willing to contribute too little. They demonstrated that people cannot produce well when their hopes for fulfillment lie in the realm of consumption.

Hard Realities

Most economists and business managers are convinced that the United States will soon be off the consumption binge. Few Americans need such news. They are well aware of (even if they don't understand) inflation, resource shortages, and a loss of competitiveness versus other nations. They feel that, somehow, they have been betrayed. They relied on the system, and the system let them down. The superconsumers no longer have the quantity or quality of goods they want. This does not mean they are all ready to get off the consumption binge, however. Some, in fact, are still hoping to get their share.

The bad news has been streaming in for years, but many of us chose to ignore it. The United States no longer holds the number one position in nearly every industry as it once did. Some of its industries are fading, some are being downsized, and even some of the newly developing industries face stiff foreign competition. In recent years, the public has heard a great deal about productivity—the ratio of the output of goods and services to the inputs of labor, capital, materials, and energy. It has heard expressions of alarm about the nation's improving its effectiveness in using these inputs at a slower and slower rate. In fact, productivity declined in 1978, 1979, and 1980. Other nations, meanwhile, have been improving their productivity faster, threatening to become more efficient than the United States.

Poor rates of improvement in productivity show up in indicators that reflect the problem in more human terms. For example, during the 1950s, the unemployment rate averaged 4.5 percent; during the 1960s, it climbed to 4.8 percent; in the 1970s, it jumped to 6.2 percent; and in the early 1980s, it averaged more than 8 percent. The prices that Americans pay for the goods they buy also reflect the productivity problem. Consumer prices rose only 22 percent in the 1950s and 26 percent in the 1960s, but they nearly doubled in the 1970s.

Despite the poor performance in productivity and the flow of imports that challenge Americans' ability to keep their jobs, workers' compensation has been rising fast. During the period 1978 to 1980, for example, compensation advanced 8.5, 9.7, and then 9.9 percent while productivity was declining. The net effect was an increase in the labor cost per unit of output and, therefore, a jump in prices and the loss of competitiveness in comparison with industries of other nations.

The negotiation of "givebacks" or future wage increases forgone by workers in the early 1980s was an attempt to roll back the disparity between U.S. labor costs and those of competitor nations. Some industries, such as steel and autos, had priced themselves out of the market through poor productivity improvement coupled with fast-rising labor costs. In the auto industry, strong union efforts had pushed hourly employment costs to a level nearly double that of the average worker in American manufacturing. Management, too, had to share the blame for giving up too much in the past and for not investing in new production technology and product improvement that would have kept the industry out in front. The situation was due in no small part to the fact that jobs were narrowly defined and generally unsatisfying. Employees were not well-informed about the economic facts of life, and they were not allowed to participate in decision making in a hierarchical, tradition-bound industry.

How long will we have to pay for the sins of the 1960s and 1970s? Several possibilities lie before us:

1. *A return to the "good old days."* That is out of the question. Our production machine was built when people were willing to deny themselves and fit into hierarchical organizations. It flourished when other industrialized nations were weakened by war, and when Third World countries were not competitive factors. Development of a

world economy and new competition for the available resources and markets force us to say good-bye to yesterday.

2. *Continued decline.* It is a possibility but not inevitable. Other nations have to be expected to rise to higher levels of industrialization and affluence, but we need not fall backwards for them to advance. What we face is the difficult task of adjusting to who we are and what we can do best.

3. *Slower economic growth.* This is the most likely possibility. Within the overall improvement, however, specific sectors will rise while others fall. Increasing competition from ascending nations will make it even more imperative that we renew our commitment to work and become more effective producers. The United States will need to maintain a delicate balance between production and consumption, and it will have to offset the forces that might push us toward social turmoil.

We cannot expect the constant upward mobility that propelled people psychologically for all this nation's history. We are more likely to see both upward and downward mobility. Children won't necessarily rise higher than their parents in educational attainment or incomes. We already see upper-middle-class parents whose children, by choice or by the realities of the job market, are not "doing as well."

If we face slower economic growth, we face the old pressures for redistributing wealth because hard times hit the poor harder than they affect the better-off, history shows. Fast economic growth didn't guarantee an egalitarian society, but it did offer sufficient upward mobility to give people hope for economic improvement. Now, a slower pace of growth or the decline of certain major business sectors could drive a wedge between people. Many have already made it clear they want tougher law enforcement, lower taxes, less government interference in economic affairs, and less government assistance to others. As people fight to preserve what they have, hostility could be expressed not only by the have-nots as in the 1960s but by the no-longer-have-as-much.

People who are making economic progress are more willing to lend a hand or let government lend a hand on their behalf. But when they perceive themselves slipping backwards either because of a more slowly growing economy or because they are in a losing sector, they are likely to display less sympathy toward others—particularly if they are self-centered and consumption-oriented. Clashes could occur between people with needs that they consider entitlements and those who embrace the idea that what you get is what you earn—the notion that so colored work attitudes earlier in this century and was sometimes confused with the Protestant ethic. We face, then, the challenge of replacing that consumption ethic with something more meaningful and more sustainable.

Work to Be Done

There will be much work to be done even though the end of American industrial supremacy is heightening the fear that there will not be enough work to go around. It may appear that the nation is running out of work, that technology is reducing the number of jobs available, and that the economy can run with less and less human input even in good times. This notion ignores two facts: (1) Technology has created new jobs and new industries, enabling us to put forty million more Americans to work in the last thirty years and thereby employ a larger percentage of the population; and (2) even if all our material needs could somehow be satisfied by machines, there are other needs to be met, other jobs to be done.

Too many visions of the future include only images of rockets and robots and the assumption that freedom and humanness will be lost to technology. But freedom and humanness are more likely to be impaired by hobbling technological innovation. Without it, people become locked into the present—economically and spiritually. They would be less free to travel and communicate. Vague visions of the long-term future in which robots do all the work and computers do all the thinking prevent us from addressing the real problems of today, the coming decades, and the long-term future. High unemployment throughout the world is a management problem—one of matching the available people to the countless unmet needs of humankind. The nations that have high unemployment also have much work to be done to improve the quality of life.

Overall, the United States may experience some easing in the pressure to create jobs since the rate of population growth is running less than in recent decades. However, a decline in the total numbers does not in itself mean pressures will ease among the employed. Although the number of persons in the 18-to-24-year-old bracket will decline between now and 1995, the middle age bracket will bulge with maturing adults from the Baby Boom. This is the age group that spends heavily and invests heavily, provided it earns well. If it is confronted with traditional, hierarchical, pyramid-shaped organizations, however, this group will create a bottleneck in the skilled, professional, and management ranks. Discontent could grow among them and among the younger people behind them since the opportunity for advancement will be tighter than ever. Management will be challenged to make work more interesting and genuinely rewarding and rely less on the quest for promotion to propel people. It will also have to create flatter organizations to eliminate the frustrations and ineffectiveness of hierarchy.

People in the upper age brackets pose a great unknown. The number past age fifty-five will grow by nine million to reach a total of fifty-five million at the end of this century. Will they become a drag on those who are employed, or will they find employment in their golden years? If they remain in the workplace, some will vie with youth for the traditional lower-level jobs while others intensify the pressures in the middle and upper ranks.

The United States faces the dual challenge of not only creating jobs but creating the right kinds of jobs—of not only providing incomes so people can consume, but providing work that, in itself, meets a variety of noneconomic needs. Forcing people back into a self-denial mode so they will accept any jobs available would match neither people's wants nor provide the commitment, inventiveness, and flexibility needed to be competitive in today's global economy.

A company or industry fighting for above-average growth in an era of slower growth will have to emphasize innovation rather than reliance on self-denial and meaningless jobs. Innovation is the child of the self-reliant. People with heads bowed in submission do not innovate. If people relinquish their individuality and creativity, the system becomes less and less adaptable—an intolerable trait for managing in times when economic growth is far from automatic.

A Look at Today's Jobs

Obsolete images of the jobs that exist prevent us from dealing properly with the problems of work. If we note what the journalists and politicians are saying, we would assume that the typical American jobholder is a blue-collar worker slaving on an assembly line. But only one out of five workers is in manufacturing establishments, and many of them wear white collars. Of the twenty-one million persons employed in manufacturing, fewer than one million are in assembly (but not necessarily assembly-line) work.

Most American workers are found in jobs outside manufacturing. Although manufacturing output has soared tremendously in recent decades, the number of workers involved in it has increased only slightly. From 1960 to 1980, while total civilian employment increased by two-thirds, manufacturing employment advanced by only one-fifth. Jobs and economic activity have grown fastest in the service sectors, which now account for a slightly larger share of gross national product than does the production of goods. Government activity alone—at the federal, state, and local levels—accounts for nearly as many jobs as all of manufacturing.

These trends lead us to assume the United States is becoming a service economy. We are moving in that direction, but we are far from being there. Many of today's service jobs (in advertising, data processing, consulting, and financial services, for example) are dependent on serving manufacturers. Many so-called information industry jobs involve the production of information goods such as books, communications equipment, and computers. Terms such as "service economy" and "information economy" may excite us and may even reflect the main thrust of economic development, but they suggest that other sectors are unimportant or nonexistent. The basic industries are going to be around for a long time.

The United States will not become a service economy by failing in manufacturing. It will get there only if it industrializes to the point where it can do a superlative job of manufacturing certain things—a transition similar to that of leaving the agrarian economy behind. The United States became a manufacturing economy not by abandoning its farms but by injecting them with so much technology that 2 percent of the workforce can now feed the nation with plenty to spare for exporting.

In manufacturing, there has been no such injection of technology. Compared to the government-aided research and information-sharing programs for agriculture, manufacturers spend relatively little of their own or government money for the development of improved manufacturing methods. Information sharing is hampered by legislation, regulation, and corporate hesitancy.

A significant number of people believe we might be better off to show less concern for traditional economic growth and tend more to our quality of life; still, the quality of life depends on first having food, shelter, transportation, and other basics. When Amitai Etzioni called attention to the need to "reindustrialize" America in 1980, he was not ignoring the importance of being concerned with the quality of life. He argued, instead, that while we might like to pursue both traditional economic growth *and* the nonmaterial aspects of life, we cannot afford to do both at once.[2] By concentrating first on rebuilding—or revitalizing—the economy, we can later afford to pursue our other interests.

Progress, Not Preservation

How can we reindustrialize or revitalize the economy? What can we do to improve our manufacturing base and get into a high-powered, redevelopment drive? One school of thought leans toward government plans or controls. It advocates selecting certain industries to support or protect. That is what President Carter and others began advocating in the closing days of his administration. Unfortunately, national programs and plans tend to lock an economy into the past rather than to open doors to the future. By propping up losing industries, no matter how vital they may seem, artificial supports weaken them in the long run; and new, potentially great industries are robbed of the resources they need to grow. What Etzioni had recommended and what the early Reagan administration advocated were broad incentives for investment, research and development, and productivity improvement. Supporters of this school of thought believe effective industries should be permitted to rise on their own strength while those that are not competitive should be allowed to shrink or disappear. Those who hold the latter view are often accused of being inattentive to the preservation of jobs. Nevertheless, it's progress, not "preservation," that creates employment. Jobs are better provided by strong, dynamic industries than by those that have to be sheltered from competition.

The terms "high technology" and "low technology" have become popular ways of referring to certain industries, and more and more people suspect we will take the high road, abandoning entire industries that are labelled "low technology." This is a superficial way of viewing the world of work and could lead to unfortunate political and economic decisions at both the national and the corporate level. In a so-called high-technology industry such as semiconductors, there are many dull, routine, low-skilled jobs. On the other hand, a low-technology or smokestack industry such as steel making employs advanced technologies—computers and telecommunications and even developments in biotechnology like the use of microbes to separate wastes from the water discharged from mills.

The United States can compete in the world market only with what it does best, and this does not include the dull, routine work—even in high-technology industries—that could either be automated away or permitted to flow to other countries. It will have to create—in both high- and low-technology industries—jobs for a highly educated workforce. Peter Drucker has pointed out that the United States is facing a decline in the number of people for entry-level jobs and manual work while other nations have millions of people begging to perform such work.[3] By allowing other nations to industrialize, we would create export markets for those things we produce here.

Drucker advocates the concept of "production sharing," whereby nations would trade what they have to offer—labor, management expertise, natural resources, technology, and markets.[4] This notion, a grandchild of Adam Smith's "comparative advantage," is more than a suggestion; it is already a major factor in world economic activity. In many industries, materials are shipped to one country for processing, on to another for intermediate manufacturing steps, still elsewhere for final assembly, and then to the final market in still other countries.

American business leaders recognize the internationalization of business. Few of them favor bailing out industries or a Lockheed or Chrysler. Although their selfish interests may rise up when their own companies are threatened with extinction, they recognize that the free enterprise system cannot work that way. Unfortunately, their loud occasional cries for protection confuse the public and the politicians. It is interesting to note, however, that the cries for protectionism were far fewer and softer in the depths of the recessions in the early 1980s than we might have expected.

Business executives are as aware as anyone that the United States cannot regain dominance in every industry. The manufacturing sector, they know, will undergo significant change in the next decade. Many changes have already taken place in recent years. For example, in the early 1970s, steel industry officials were trying to figure how to close the gap between what they could produce and what American consumers needed. Since then, they have given up trying to finance enough expansion to meet all domestic needs. In the face of foreign competition, they have, instead, shut down many of their facilities. The auto industry, some experts predict, will be concentrated among six or seven world manufacturers by the 1990s and no more than two of these manufacturers may be based here.

In newer industries such as aerospace, communications equipment, and computers, the United States enjoyed an early lead. But other nations are making it a matter of concentrated national effort to erase that lead. American companies enjoy a head start in biotechnology, perhaps the next giant industry, but the challenge from abroad is already being felt.

There are no certainties as to what the United States will or will not produce in the future. The future is for us to determine. On the surface, there are four determinants of where manufacturing takes place:

1. *Resources.* The United States has many of the raw materials for production, but it has to import a significant portion of many key items. More and more nations are insisting on injecting some labor content before exporting their natural riches. In the future, the American companies may be forced to do more manufacturing (or allow more to be done) in the nations with the natural resources.

2. *Markets.* America's best market is its own people, but the effect of imports has to be offset by selling abroad. Sometimes, American firms seeking to share in the growing markets of other nations often lack access unless they manufacture there. Even without artificial barriers, we can export little to the less developed nations if they don't have dollars to exchange or a sufficiently developed economy to require the kinds of goods we produce; helping them build a manufacturing sector creates a better market for us. All this suggests the United States will continue to increase its investments in manufacturing abroad.

3. *Workers.* This country has traditionally been on the short side in skilled manpower. That's why it has been able to absorb millions of immigrants while showing an eagerness to mechanize and automate. With a shortage of skilled workers and a decreasing supply of young people to take entry-level jobs in the years ahead, both unskilled and skilled work will drift overseas.

4. *Capital.* Manufacturers always complain that they don't have enough capital for expansion and modernization while the financial community assures them that there will be enough. Whatever the supply of capital, we know its suppliers are fickle; they put their money where returns are likely to be greatest. Increasingly, capital is crossing national boundaries. Americans invest a great deal abroad, and foreigners' investments in the United States have been on the rise. Where things are manufactured depends less and less on where the capital originates.

This leaves us, then, with natural resources, markets, and workers to worry about or do something about when it comes to determining where manufacturing is located. And these factors are, essentially, *people.* Resources are determined by people both through the products they demand (which establishes the value of things) and through their inventiveness (which can make some substance a usable, desirable "resource"). Markets, obviously, are people—the consuming side of them. Workers are people, too—the producing side of them. Whether the United States manufactures and what it manufactures, therefore, will depend not on outside factors so much as on the ways in which its people produce, invest, and consume. If Americans make the proper response to changing global economics and shifts in industries' relative strengths, there is no reason to write off manufacturing as a source of jobs for them.

Working on the Infrastructure

There is still another essential ingredient for a healthy economy: infrastructure. That term became a buzzword in 1983 as Americans were made aware of the sad state of decay of their bridges, roads, railways and other public facilities—an estimated three trillion dollar replacement challenge. The restoration of our infrastructure could provide many thousands of jobs for many years for people of diverse skills and interests.

Whenever I enter Manhattan and see the massive bridges, the Empire State Building, the subways, and miles of streets, I am impressed by the tremendous infrastructure that was erected there long ago. The congestion, decay, and disrepair overwhelm me when I think of what it would take to restore or replace what I see. Traveling along interstate highways, I see long stretches being rebuilt—highways that hardly seem to have been finished. More than 8000 miles of the nations' 42,000 mile interstate highway system needs to be overhauled. One of every five bridges needs major rework or replacement. Major urban areas will have to raise approximately $100 billion in the next century to maintain their water systems.[5] As many as half of the communities in the United States may not be able to allow any significant economic expansion because of their limited facilities for water and waste treatment.

Much of our infrastructure was built by low-paid, immigrant laborers whose work was a source of pride, inspiration, and hope for the generations to come. Their bridges and buildings were testimonies to man's spirit of adventure. We now face a maintenance and replacement chore—unless we can once again make that challenge a source of pride. For many workers, this massive project could provide tangible results for their efforts—something with which they could identify. Public buildings, dams, railways, subways, airports, and housing could be their contribution to a rebuilt, reborn America. However, we have to back off from our compulsion to consume, be willing to invest in the long term, and find satisfaction in creating and restoring.

Nothing in the Package

Many of today's jobs do not provide a tangible product that one can admire or point to for others to see. For many, work is paperwork. In 1900, clerical workers—secretaries, bookkeepers, and tellers (only 200,000 of them!) constituted less than 1 percent of the labor force. Today, numbering more than 14 million, they hold about one out of seven jobs.

This trend to "knowledge work" has not been especially uplifting. The keypuncher's job is safer and cleaner than those of the miners and heavy industry workers at the turn of the century, but it represents the replacement of mental toil for physical toil. The shift from a predominance of blue-collar workers to white-collar workers in the 1950s did not signify that millions of people had risen to higher paying, more challenging jobs. In fact, many clerical workers and even some lower-level supervisors have not fared so well financially as have skilled craftsmen and members of strong labor unions. The relative improvement in average blue-collar pay is also partly due to the fact that many of the laborer positions have disappeared while the number of skilled workers and foremen in the goods-producing industries has increased as equipment and organizations have grown more complex.

Future developments in the office will resemble those that have already taken place in the factory. At the turn of the century, factory laborers far outnumbered managers and professionals. Since then, the number of managers and other indirect workers has risen dramatically in relation to the number of production workers. In the years ahead, many white-collar and pink-collar jobs will either be automated out or upgraded into positions demanding inputs of greater education and the exercise of greater creativity and flexibility.

Growth in white-collar work has been a female phenomenon to a large degree. Entrance of women into the work force is not new, but the pace has been accelerating. The number of working women has doubled since 1950. Half of all married women are now at work outside the home compared with only one-third in 1960 and only one out of twenty at the turn of the century. Of Americans employed today, about 44 percent are women. By the year 2000, women will account for half of the workforce.

Until now, the heavy influx of women into the labor force reflected both the push of high consumption and the pull exerted by the development of lower-level, white-collar positions. Some women came to work as primary breadwinners while others were out to supplement their husbands' income because their families were hooked on high expectations that one breadwinner couldn't satisfy. Employers welcomed these willing candidates for undemanding assignments in food services, electronics assembly, and paperwork processing.

Now that the doors are open wide to women, more and more of them are looking for a greater commitment in their work. They want to do more and be more. They want careers, not just jobs. They want to be engineers, advertising executives, department managers, and company presidents. And their special problems with divided family responsibilities are putting pressure on employers to make changes in the way work is packaged—in working hours, the number of working days per week, and even in the location of work.

New Work Packages

The use of staggered working hours, flexitime, compressed workweeks, job-sharing, work-sharing, permanent part-time work, and other new packages of work is spreading throughout American business. The Work in America Institute estimates that one out of five workers is now affected by new work schedules and that one-half will be by 1990.[6] These new work packages meet special needs of both men and women as well as certain employers by eliminating the disruptive clash of personal needs with work routines and enabling persons to lead more integrated lives that include a meaningful commitment to their work. They enable some employers to balance work flow better and win most employers a less dissatisfied, more productive workforce.

Some companies are experimenting with allowing certain jobs to be performed at home since computer and communications technology enables clerical and professional people to be in touch with the office or factory from home or other remote location. Although there will be growth in this practice, a relatively small percentage of workers will communicate rather than commute to work if the nature of their work does not require direct contact with others and they prefer to remain at home.

The Future of Work

Some of the work to be done in the near future does look glamorous or, at least, attractive. However, it is premature to regard the United States as a post-industrial society and to assume that we are on the threshold of an era when all jobs become nonroutine and challenge people's mental limits. Technological advances have created many high-discretion jobs. They are creating new industries or changing existing ones in ways that call for workers with greater self-control, creativity, problem-solving skills, and decision-making capabilities. But they have not eliminated all the routine work or all the physical work.

With the monumental amount of work to be done to restore United States manufacturing capability, rebuild the infrastructure, and meet the demand for more and more services, we will need a diverse workforce. We will need engineers and we will need laborers. We will need an infinite mix of strength, dexterity, and intelligence. For a long time to come, we will have work for people along the entire continuum of abilities and interests.

For the foreseeable future, we will see jobs come and go in various industries. The best job security will come not through attempts to stop these dynamics but by preparing people to flow with them—to acquire the adaptability to venture from disappearing jobs in one company or sector to emerging jobs in another. In the August 1983 strike against AT&T, the Communications Workers of America won company-paid training and relocation assistance to help workers who might face layoffs—something they feared in light of fast technological change and the restructuring of the company. This was an important new approach to seeking career security rather than traditional job security or job preservation.

Along with developing attitudes that will permit people to make job changes during their career, we will also need to restore the respectability of any job well done. We have glorified mundane white-collar jobs while degrading other jobs that create essential products and services. In a quest for status, we have encouraged people to scramble for jobs for which they may be underqualified despite their credentials which give them the illusion of being overqualified. In effect, we have elevated a *job ethic* over the work ethic, robbing people of the significance that good performance at any job might have given them. Using the job as a position for self-gratification or winning the esteem of others leads neither to genuine fulfillment nor to being a good producer. It is merely another form of consumption.

People are troubled because they see the prospects for less economic gain than they would like and because, at the same time, they suspect that economic gain alone is not enough to fulfill them. They are frustrated not only with the economic indicators but the human indicators of "depression." They realize they cannot hope, even under the best of conditions, to attain sufficient earning power to purchase the kinds of human services that only caring people can provide one another.

We should waste no more time wondering if there is enough work to be done. We must ask, instead, how we can manage all the work—how we can match it with what people can do and want to do. If we make the work itself rewarding to the jobholder, we will be also be well on our way to attending to quality-of-life considerations. If we think not only in terms of the usual concept of "full employment" but in terms of fully employing each individual to his or her potential, we will reduce the chances of suffering that "going backwards" feeling. Human growth and economic growth will proceed together, elevating the individual far more than did the consumption ethic or the job ethic. Then we will begin to displace the consumption ethic with something better. We will enable people to become well-balanced consumers and producers, reasonably content with the present, yet eager to meet the future.

We need not long for some distant future when everyone will be employed at self-actualizing work on some high plane of intellectual activity. We can begin the process of human development now with the tasks before us.

6

Whirlwind
of Changing Values

CONCEPTS OF PRODUCING AND CONSUMING HAVE CHANGED DRAMATICALLY over the years, taking American workers from a Protestant ethic with strong social and spiritual implications to a consumption ethic and a job ethic, neither of which allowed the individual any meaning in terms outside his own economic interests. Fundamental changes are occurring once again in American values, however, and they have begun to lay the foundation for an entirely new view of work.

One of the major changes is the growing realization that the United States has to become some sort of *conserver society*. Facing slower economic growth and a tighter supply of materials and energy, Americans are convinced that they cannot maintain a high-consumption economy. They will have to do the same with less or more with less.

Working with less does not necessarily mean living "worse," however. In fact, people might become more alive and meet more of their human needs if they dedicated themselves to producing rather than consuming. The business community could help by turning its persuasive powers to inducing people to buy resource-responsible products and help cultivate a producer mentality rather than treating people primarily as consuming mechanisms.

A significant number of Americans already indicate they are willing to accept a slower rate of economic growth. One major survey showed that 54 percent of Americans believe that maintaining a high rate of economic growth should not be given a high priority. At the same time, 49 percent favor a slower rate of economic growth in order to protect the environment. Over two-thirds believe that more stress should be placed on teaching people to live with basic essentials than on reaching a high standard of living.[1] The study concludes: "A utilization ethic is deeply embedded in the minds of Americans and has been so since the earliest days of the nation. A conservationist ethic, which is a relatively new factor in American life, has become equally pervasive in our present-day outlook."[2]

Greater world-awareness and understanding of some of the scientific facts of life are tempering the old "utilization" or consumption ethic. The newer conservationist values are not harbored only in the hearts of a few people dedicated to preserving nature, protecting the environment, or fighting world hunger. "The narrower, 'environmentalist' perspective, with its focus on the 'single issues' of pollution, conservation, and population growth, has broadened and stimulated a large segment of our citizenry to think in terms of the finiteness and fragility of the world," the study finds.[3]

Especially significant for the future is the finding that the conservationist view is strongest in the 18-to-34 age group and lowest among people 50 and over who were not sensitized to environmental considerations in their formative years. It also increases with people's level of education. In a maturing population that emphasizes higher education, therefore, we can expect the conservationist view to grow stronger in the years ahead. This represents a significant departure from the American tradition of assuming man must master nature. With the rise of science in the seventeenth century, says Jeremy Rifkin in *The Emerging Order*, "nature, once seen as divine, magnificent and mysterious, was transformed into so much quantitative physical phenomena. . . ."[4] With God removed, nature became fair game for man's exploitation.

In America, more than anywhere else, man became master of his own destiny in an exaltation of independence and rugged individualism. Now, however, many people see themselves as stewards of the planet—a concept in harmony with the exhortations of *The Book of Genesis*. Whether for selfish or unselfish reasons, they recognize the world's interdependencies and the fact that people everywhere have shared concerns. More and more Americans—not just the young or the radical—are embracing an *ecology ethic* to one degree or another. Some are concerned about their own health or that of the generations to come. Some are concerned about preserving the planet either for the enjoyment of man or on behalf of all forms of life.

Science in Perspective

When science was spawned out of philosophy—the study of life's big questions—it dealt only with the "how" of the physical universe. However, in time, it came to be regarded as the ultimate source of truth for many people. To them, if something couldn't be measured, if it couldn't be quantified, it either didn't exist or it didn't matter.

Twentieth-century America was the epitome of the elevation of science in the public mind. This was a nation that demanded much and received much from technological innovation, but now it knows that there are limits to what technology can do. There are signs that people are expecting less of technology, that they are tempering their demands for a risk-free life. They have learned that anything from saccharin to sunshine may cause cancer. They know that, even when used with the best of intentions, technology cannot guarantee that some adverse effects will not occur. People are now more willing to examine the trade-offs of any proposed technological innovation. They have begun to reconcile themselves to limits.

The problems posed by the power of today's science and technology have caused people to raise once again the "why" questions. As a result, they are beginning to put science and technology back into a larger context. They are turning inward or outward to find what man is and what he should do with his new-found powers. The late biologist Rene Dubos wrote that "man wishes to add deeper significance to his endeavors." Man, he said, has begun to search within himself for "a kind of satisfaction he has not found so far in his conquest of the external world."[5] Theologian Hans Kung points out that, today, "practically all the important contemporary scientists . . . are well aware how little science is able to answer questions about the meaning of human existence, about the value of life and about our moral duties."[6]

Science itself is losing some of the certainty that has generally characterized it. When I was in high school we were taught that the hard rock foundation of the material world consisted of electrons, protons, and neutrons. Since then, there has been not only a proliferation in the number of subatomic particles that we believe exist, but scientists now tell us that matter is really a form of energy.

"When we observe the particles that make up atoms, we never see any substance; what we observe are continually changing dynamic patterns—a perpetual dance of energy," says physicist–author Fritjof Capra. Even mind and matter no longer seem to be separate categories. This changes the whole way we view man's relationship to nature, he says.[7]

We can regard the interest in ecology and conservation as merely matters of survival or good behavior. But the interest is, in many cases, a matter of an individual's sensing that he or she has to participate in a greater unity whether it be strictly human or human and divine. There is a sense that the individual is part of a greater whole just as the electron is—that, perhaps, we are really more akin to energy forms.

Bringing our views of science into proper perspective does not mean we have to totally discredit it. There is no reason for science to split with theology or for an individual to abandon reason and rationality for nonrational thinking. It was unfortunate that the Church opposed science from the beginning, says Hans Kung. The failure of Christian theology and the Church to ally with science "contributed substantially to the establishment of both scientific and political atheism. . . ."[8]

Bringing scientific thinking into better balance with nonscientific relates to the substantial amount of current study and discussion of the functions of the brain's right and left hemispheres. Many experts conclude that we depend too heavily on the left side with its scientific, rational approach to knowing. They believe that there are certain situations, especially in a complex world, that call for intuitive, nonlinear thinking which enables us to grasp the wholeness of things. Some believe that through the right side of his brain man can even tap into some universal power. The left hemisphere won't be abandoned, but the right hemisphere will be given more play since it promises to be more effective in dealing with the growing complexities of life.

Unfortunately, the quest for certainty causes some people to turn their backs on science just as people once turned their backs to religion because science promised a greater certainty in some matters. Fundamentalist, antiscience thinking gained momentum during the late 1970s and early 1980s and captured a great deal of national attention and some political power. It has even managed the enactment of legislation enforcing the teaching of—or at least commentary on—"creation science" alongside the theory of evolution in some schools.

Instead of allowing their spiritual awareness to guide the use of science and technology to solve humankind's physical problems, some people choose to deny science. In so doing, they reject man's ability to create, interpret, and inquire. Theirs seems to be a religion of despair rather than one of hope. In effect, they advocate inaction—waiting for this miserable world to end. To the degree that they block the pursuit of knowledge, they can fall victim to superstition. To the degree that they resist the full use of knowledge, they restrict their ability to put love fully into action.

While science cannot answer all our questions, it can help us humanize life. In fact, it can help us be more fully human. It can help us pursue a nobility of purpose in taking responsibility for the planet far beyond what was possible when man had illusions of dominating nature in order to serve only economic or technological imperatives. If a Protestant or Christian ethic is to shape our concepts of purposeful work once again, the faithful will have to involve themselves in the material world and bring the transcendental dimension to it. Christianity can be a force in the world of work or become irrelevant. It can provide lessons of love and fellowship or curl up in self concern and elitism. It can teach the beauty of life's mysteries or repel people who don't want to have them explained away.

The Rise of Spirituality

Both within the established churches and outside them today, there is a surge—or resurgence—of spirituality. Central to the ethical milieu swirling around us is a sense that the material world is not all there is—that fellowship is important—that man must have some transcendental connection. We aren't likely to see a radical departure from material interests to a life of contemplation, but we may see a totally new way of viewing the material world.

Much of the rise in spirituality is reflected outside the traditional measures, however. In 1979, 61 percent of the U.S. population was listed as members of established churches. That compares with slightly less in 1950 (57 percent) and more (64 percent) in 1960.[9] These numbers do not reflect any surge in church attendance, but they could mask a greater spiritual awareness and commitment among church attenders. The new spirituality can be seen not only in developments such as neopentacostalism within the church but in new religious cults, meditation, and even the books and films on the supernatural. There is widespread effort to find meaning—to find something that defies the concrete, quantifiable, rational definition of the world. At the same time, there has been a rush of interest in diet, exercise, and holistic medicine. People are turning inward, reaching outward, and struggling upward. Much of the activity is through experiential pursuit in which the individual disregards the social constructs and any church intermediation to seek reality directly.

In general, the "quest for individual spiritual meaning and for caring relationships has replaced both the older dogmatic religion and the nihilism of the mid-twentieth century," says Willis Harman.[10] More and more people tend to pick and choose their beliefs; not satisfied with a particular "religion," they prefer to fashion their own spirituality. It is interesting to note that sales of religious books nearly quadrupled over the 1970s; they account for slightly more than one out of ten dollars in book sales.[11]

After centuries of being challenged by rationalism and scientific thinking, the traditional churches are now encountering the influence of Eastern, meditative disciplines and other means of seeking direct religious experience. Direct, personal experience is emphasized in such activities as Zen meditation, body expression and massage classes, and Christians' speaking in tongues. It is manifested in church groups employing folk music, banners, and ritual chanting. It is seen in encounter sessions and biofeedback techniques.[12]

What are the reasons for this striving for peak experiences or spiritual "highs?" Some possibilities: Religion is being used as an escape from the world; people are resorting to "magical" means for doing better in the material world; some are genuinely searching for a supreme being and an understanding of our relationship to him and whatever that may entail in terms of a role in this world; God is getting in touch with us—the contact emanates from without.

Perhaps all these factors are at work within people. We cannot fully determine the reasons for the increasing spirituality, but we do have to ask what the results will be. Will they lead to greater commitment to the world or an escape from it? Will spirituality prepare people for relationships with others and the material world or will it create apathy? On the one hand, spirituality may be used in a desperate attempt to win physical comforts in much the same manner as was done with the distorted Protestant ethic. Sociologist Marvin Harris views the movement skeptically. He believes that, rather than being a triumph over consumerism and materialism, it is a last-ditch effort to attain material wealth and cope with world problems through magical means.[13] If this movement is genuine spirituality but too inward in its focus, it could result in people's refusal to deal directly with problems in the physical world.

On the other hand, if spirituality turns people outward, they will approach their work, their interpersonal relationships, and their institutions with different expectations than people have in recent decades. Spiritual awareness would heighten our consciousness of moral problems posed by being in the world and provide the strength to work through them. It need not merely make us feel good, give us magical solutions to worldly problems, or set down simple answers to the mysteries of life.

These developments are not just abstractions for the theologian or sociologist to contemplate. They are a central part of the hard realities with which managers are confronted in the workplace. Managers must see people in their full measure if they are to understand where people are coming from and where they are going. People are looking for meaning. They are frequently looking for some transcendent value—something beyond this material world. It would be self-defeating for management to ignore this fundamental truth because it has to know through whom it is working and for whom. In earlier times and in other places, man has regarded his animal or material needs as low or evil and his spiritual needs as supreme. Modern America turned the relationship upside down, regarding economic matters as essential and spiritual concerns as secondary. If people are, in fact, rearranging their economic and noneconomic priorities, management will face dramatic change in people's attitudes toward the goods and services they consume and in their regard for their role as producers.

The Drive for Unity

While the ancient Greek concepts viewing the body as bad and the spirit as good have been enfolded into many religions, one of the new strains of spirituality—evolutionary theology—regards the two as sacred and developing together. Teilhard de Chardin, the Jesuit paleontologist whose profound writings have done so much to resolve theology with evolutionary theory, stands as the "patron saint" of many of the leading thinkers in this movement. In this view of evolution, the world is progressing to higher and higher and more complex forms. This is not a random or accidental progression but one driven by an inner force.

If the debate over evolutionary theory has been heated up to now, such thinking could really stir it to a boil. More and more people, coming from different directions, are speaking of the evolution of a universal consciousness which will shake the foundations of individualism and old concepts of self. Buckminster Fuller believed, for example, that we are evolving from the phase of separate individuals and nations to an interrelated, global system. Man is capable of much greater cooperation than he has shown up to now, Fuller said.[14] Physicist Fritjof Capra says: "The material world, according to contemporary physics, is not a mechanical system composed of separate objects, but instead appears as a complex web of relationships."[15] Hans Kung, like Chardin, has asserted: "God is not a supramundane being, above the clouds, in the physical heaven. The naive, anthropomorphic idea is obsolete." God "does not operate above the world process, but *in* the world process; in, with and among human beings and things."[16]

Some who feel the sweep of evolution believe that a broad network of individuals will attain breakthroughs in consciousness and cause a major leap upward in evolution. Humankind, in fact, will be a partner in bringing about its own evolution. We are moving into a state of cocreativeness, says Barbara Marx Hubbard. "We are at the dawn of conscious evolution." At the 1982 assembly of the World Future Society she said, "We are at the threshold of the greatest moral revolution the world has ever seen. We are concerned about ending war. We are concerned with preserving other species. We in the U.S. can ask. 'What's after materialism?' because we have been there. That's why we will be the first spiritual nation."

The concept of coevolution reflects a deep respect for the universe and for man. Although it holds that the spirit will ultimately prevail and the material world will wither away, it is not escapist. Driven by excitement with the highest pursuits of the mind and compassion for the mundane problems of the physical world, it attempts to rekindle man's sense of responsibility. An understanding of the evolutionary view of the world creates opportunities for the old faith, says Kung. Opportunities lie in "a deeper understanding of God—not above or outside but in the midst of the world and its evolution; a deeper understanding of creation—not as contrary to evolution but as making evolution possible; a deeper understanding of the special position of man. . . ."[17]

The "old faith," has not been in the lead in ecological or social concern; those who are engaged in traditional religious activities are more likely to place high priority on material matters. The growing number of conservation-minded people are less likely to be involved in traditional religious practices. The current sweep of spirituality, then, may pose a threat to traditional religion. On the other hand, the rising sense of unity may either bring together and strengthen the now divergent bodies of religious beliefs or convince people that diversity can and should exist within unity.

The search for a transcendental connection definitely poses a threat to traditional secular organizations, however. New concepts of individualism and interdependence will confound the leader who does not understand the important subtleties in today's values shift. "The spirit of our age is fraught with paradox," warns Marilyn Ferguson. "It is at the same time pragmatic and transcendental. It values both enlightenment and mystery—power and humility—interdependence and individuality."[18]

A New View of Man

Both the fundamentalist and the evolutionist forms of religion are departures from total reliance on rational thinking. The first emphasizes prerational thought processes. The latter attempts to make a transition to something beyond, but also including, the rational process. Even scientists—perhaps we should say *especially* scientists—have come to realize that the material world is not a simple mechanical system made up of separate parts. As people become more aware of the interrelationships around them, they may well work toward tapping into a greater unity. They will try to find the unified whole in any particular field of study and in all of life itself; then, they will seek to experience the sense of oneness with the world.

A profound shift is, therefore, occurring in the way people view themselves. They already know that they are more than economic units, and they suspect they are more than bundles of physical needs. They are searching for a new and broader definition of what it means to be human. Willis Harman has listed five fundamental images of man that have been used in this century alone: (1) a mechanism that responds to physical stimuli; (2) an animal whose instincts are modified by social forces; (3) a free being with self-awareness, reason, and free choice; (4) God's creation with freedom as well as responsibility to act according to God's will; and (5) a transcendental being with the Divine within him.[19] Harman's point is that man is far too complex to be expressed in any single image. Man is all of these images and more.

In the world of business, however, people are still being treated primarily as response mechanisms. Responding to the old economic image of man, employers try to manipulate people by providing the right stimuli such as monetary rewards for workers and sex appeal for customers who buy the right toothpaste or sports car. But these tactics lose their effectiveness when people are developing an expanded image of themselves. Marilyn Ferguson sees the overall transition adding up to a set of positive values that has to do with growth and trust. She includes the movement from comfort to concern for meaning and ambiguity, from self-control to the search for self-knowledge, from permanence to potential, from information to insight, and from power over others to sharing power.

For more than a decade, American values have been headed in this direction. In the early 1970s, the late Carl Madden, a social economist, detected some of these changes. Among them he saw a shift from more to better, from exploiting nature to living in harmony with it, from centralism to pluralism and diversity, from "work as a sacrifice to work as purposive and self-fulfilling."[20]

People's values are becoming increasingly dependent on what goes on inside them rather than on outward stimuli, says Arnold Mitchell of SRI International. Having spent more than twenty years developing what he calls a "Values and Life Styles" profile of Americans, he estimates that only about one-tenth of the population is need-driven; these people are "survivors" and "sustainers." About 70 percent of adult Americans are what he calls "belongers, emulators, or achievers"; they respond primarily to what others think of them. But he has made the important discovery that about one out of five Americans take an inner-directed route; this group includes the self-oriented, those committed to a rich inner life, and those who are societally conscious. They do not seem to be affected by the dependencies fostered by so many of our organizations. In the years ahead, says Mitchell, the proportion of inner-directed people will grow. As more inner-directed people become models for others, both young and old will increasingly select this course.

Placing science into a broader perspective, heightened regard for ecology and the conservation of resources, the rise of spirituality, and new images of man constitute more than a modification of the past. Taken together, they are revolutionary. They are the ingredients of a new paradigm—a whole new way of defining ourselves and the world. This new paradigm in itself contains diverse values, and the transition to it will be a period of tension between old and new values as well. We are entering a period during which we will have to sort out matters of taste and preference, those things on which there must be widespread agreement—a "social ethic," and certain concepts which seem to be universally true—moral imperatives.

New evidence, says Daniel Yankelovich, shows that America is evolving a new "ethic of commitment." Preoccupation with the self was a false start toward self-fulfillment, he says. Interest is shifting away from self toward connectedness with people, objects, places, projects, experiences, and achievement.[21] This new ethic of commitment is developing along two lines: (1) building closer and deeper relationships and (2) dropping conventional signs of success in favor of a more satisfying sense of personal achievement. In addition, it will incorporate some of the old values with the new. It will preserve political freedom, appreciation of attaining well-being through one's own efforts, and respectability; and it will add diversity of life-style, adventure, leisure, self-expression, and regard for the mystery and sacredness of life.[22]

The Search for Quality

A search for reality, one's true identity, and authenticity means that quality will become important in all aspects of living. People will seek quality in their relationships with one another and in the products and services they exchange with one another. To them, the inherent quality of goods and services will become more important than the status value. The products that people select will have to fulfill their intended purpose.

Quality production can come only from people who are able to commit to the product and the customer. In other words, those who manage work must look beyond the quantitative measures and build in qualitative values. If, in fact, they are going to be doing business in a conserver society, they will have to put high priorities on quality, durability, and repairability of the goods they produce. They will not be able to afford mediocrity.

Business management will have to help lead the way in reinforcing the growing appreciation for quality. That poses a monumental reeducation job in a nation sold on junk food and disposable products. The destructive models of consumers and producers conveyed in our movies, literature, TV shows, and advertising will have to be replaced with more constructive models. The education sector, also, has a key role to play in the elevation of excellence and quality. As a sector that has been ravaged by the forces for equality, it will not find it easy to instill an appreciation for the inequality in things and ideas.

The demand for quality is already challenging the assumption that bigger is better. Large organizations are sometimes able to effect economies of scale for cost reduction, but that is only one objective they must serve. Where the level of technology and the capital inputs for a product or service are high, they may be an important consideration. In much of manufacturing and virtually all of the services industries, however, the economies of smallness are often equally or more important because the closer one approaches a one-on-one relationship, the better the customer is served. Technologically, we are acquiring the capability to take many things from large scale to small, human scale. Many of the potential new energy sources, for example, point toward decentralized production. In the steel industry, the small "mini-mills" have proven highly competitive in certain product lines. Regardless of the technology involved, some manufacturers limit the size of their plants so that managers can have a firsthand awareness of what is going on and workers can communicate better with one another.

The Dispersal of Power

Today's search for wholeness or oneness will not necessarily lead to the creation of monolithic structures aimed at enforcing a oneness and sameness. In fact, the new values favor decentralization and dispersal of power. The United States has evolved into a highly diverse society—so diverse that too many decisions are made in response to pressures by people acting under a burden of information overload. Sometimes decision makers respond to the majority's wishes. Sometimes they respond to special-interest groups. They seldom, however, make what everone agrees is the best decision.

The forces for decentralization and dispersal of power are challenging our old decision-making mechanisms. People are clamoring for more direct influence in national decisions than they get from an occasional trip to the ballot box. Majority rule isn't good enough when a society blossoms into an infinite array of wants and has the technological capability of effecting earthshaking change. It doesn't work well with today's splintered political parties and the mushrooming of special-interest groups. A 51-to-49 split on the issue of building a nuclear power plant is not acceptable, no matter which side wins. The same is true of decisions regarding genetic manipulation or a host of other values issues that have far-reaching implications. We need to work our way through to consensus, allowing as many inputs as possible and arriving at a course of action with which the preponderance of people can agree. As yet, however, we lack the mechanisms for teaching people consensus-building skills.

A move away from centralization is called for not only because people want a direct hand in making decisions but because giant, centralized institutions cannot carry out the actions that are agreed upon. Although Americans once expected more and more from their institutions, they now see that there is a limit to the breadth and depth of what institutions can do for them. They are beginning to look less to institutions and more to themselves to meet their wants. An increasing proportion of people are going into business for themselves. Millions are caught up in personal health care, depending less on doctors and drugs. Some may feel they are not ready to be self-reliant, but they recognize the need to take more things into their own hands.

People want to be involved in the decision-making process at least in the setting of major objectives. Numerous regional, state, and municipal bodies have begun involving a substantial portion of their citizenry in considering alternatives for the future and setting goals or priorities. Lay persons consider the facts, but more importantly, they share their values and aspirations. In a parallel development, some workers are being involved in their companies' decision making through various forms of participative management.

Although we may presently lack the skills and the processes for making good decisions, we are working on it. "The will to build a better society . . . survives, along with the traditions of localism, self-help, and community action that only need the vision of a new society, a decent society, to give them vigor," says Christopher Lasch in *The Culture of Narcissism*.[23]

A Warmer View of the Future

Historian Robert Nisbet has observed that it is a Western tradition to envision a perfect society and to have faith in human knowledge—especially in the sciences and technology. However, he says this faith in progress is waning because of "the erosion of all the fundamental intellectual and spiritual premises upon which the idea of progress has rested throughout its long history."[24] According to Nisbet, the idea of progress grew out of the Western religions.

The strictly scientific view of the world has bred pessimism through the concept of entropy, from which some people conclude that the world is running down. But this notion could be displaced by a new sense of progress—of evolution or genesis. Rather then seeing the world as a machine that is wearing out, we could view it as a living, learning, and growing organism. We could, then, regard humankind as improvable, if not perfectible.

A more positive view of the future comes from the conviction that the individual has far more potential than has ever been realized. In the past, undue concern for individuality and for rights has often resulted in increased dependence on others through relationships based, not on caring, but on hostility—a parasitic dependence with little respect for one another. A sense of becoming and a vision of unity, however, could lead people toward a healthy interdependence that would require only a minimum of third-party or governmental intervention.

The way we perceive the future is an important determinant of what we get. Just a few years ago, it was popular for futurists to see the future in cold, rational, calculating, computer-controlled terms. More and more are now speaking of man's rising above the hardware and using it to humanize life. Rather than a bland, uniform world, they see beauty in the potential diversity. They are no longer so enjoined against technology as the major threat to man. They are coming to regard it as a tool for defining and dealing with values issues. Once seen as the big stick that will beat us into submission, technology now seems to be the vaulter's pole that will help us lift ourselves to new heights economically, socially, politically, and spiritually. It could provide the mechanisms by which people could shape the future—by which the individual can make a difference.

At the fourth general assembly of the World Future Society in 1982, I sensed a dramatic change compared to the second assembly seven years earlier. Under the theme "Communications and the Future," considerable discussion was devoted to establishing networks through which people dedicated to doing something about the future and dealing with specific problems might be in constant communication with one another. This was not a hardware show although the hardware was available to fashion vast networks of communications with either positive or negative impacts on society. Speakers and attendees displayed a new resolve to do something about the future. For many of them, word processors, data transmission, and management information systems are workaday tools. Their concern is how to use this technology to human advantage. In just seven years' time, there had been a dramatic shift from cowering at the potentially harmful uses of technology to giving full support to technology's potential positive influences on social and spiritual wellness.

I saw a similar change over the series of Woodlands Conferences on Growth. The first, in 1975, focused on the physical limits to growth. By the third, in 1979, emphasis had shifted to the social and political limits that will dictate how physical and human resources will be used. The fourth conference, in 1982, dealt with the day-to-day actions of the private sector that can contribute to a sustainable society that produces both economic and human growth. From an antibusiness undercurrent at the first conference dialogue had turned to a positive attempt to bring business in as a part of the solution to human problems.

These more recent conferences typify the confidence needed to recapture the future. From all sides comes the message that one's self-interest is bound with the interest of others—that the individual and humankind are evolving together—that the future will be exciting because change can take place in each of us and be caused by each of us.

The socioeconomic problems of the world are so complex, so many, and so interrelated that hope for the future lies only in the possible breakthrough in man's perception of himself and a leap upward in ways of knowing and understanding. We could be at the threshold of the next step in evolution as great as the rise from instincts to faith and reason—to powers of the mind that embrace these and more.

The concepts of unity and coevolution do not support the old values of rugged individualism and competition. They elevate both the individual and the community to new heights. They are tearing apart traditional packages of beliefs about man and his work which have prevented people from bringing their spiritual lives and their worklives together. They are overturning past notions of organization, control, incentives, work structure, and corporate purpose. The entire new ethical milieu in which we find ourselves points to a future of purposeful action. It sets the foundation for a dramatically new work ethic.

7

From Fantasyland
to Fulfillment

THE PROTESTANT ETHIC WAS MACHINED AWAY by advancing industrialization. Its perversion to materialism and an ethic of consumption has proven insufficient and unsustainable because people consume more than they produce if they attempt to satisfy too many of their needs through consumption.

Leaving the fantasyland of consumption where they didn't find the fulfillment they wanted, more and more people are exploring their powers of self-reliance and creativity, and they are searching for connectedness—something to which to commit their talents. They may now be ready to get off the consumption binge, and work is where they should find satisfaction of the wants that are driving them most. If the mainstream economy can turn to meet people where they are in their values, the workplace could nurture a producer mentality that would bear both material and nonmaterial fruit.

The old "great American dream" was to "move up." Ironically, it generally meant a person had to surrender many values of personal importance. The emerging new dream is based on each person's moving up in his or her own terms—a markedly different goal. We are now seeing a self-fulfillment ethic—an ethic that is still concerned with the self but which has the chance of becoming more genuinely fulfilling to the individual and more supportive of the community or society. "The question," says Amitai Etzioni, "is not whether one seeks self-fulfillment, but whether one seeks it in avenues that are constructive for self, mutuality, and community—or in ways that disregard or undermine all these."[1] Daniel Yankelovich has observed that many of the self-fulfillment activities being pursued today are self-development; they are constructive, not simply pleasure-seeking.[2] The question then becomes "What are people doing with their self-development?" Will they see themselves as the center of the universe or as part of some unity?

The drive for fulfillment seems threatened by hard economic realities. But this does not mean we will return to the good old work ethic. If people can find opportunities for growth in their work rather than having to deny their wholeness and seek solace in consumption, they could restore vigor to the economy. Economic well-being would be a by-product of people's quest for self-fulfillment since their search would be conducted in the realm of producing where they can grow and feel productive rather than in the fantasyland of consumption where they have sought solace and escape. Integrating work and nonwork life would begin to restore the individual and the community. Ironically, by attending to human growth considerations first, we would find the route to sound economic growth.

Henry Ford believed that paying his workers a good wage would make them customers for his cars, and he was right. America has built its economy on good wages and mass production. Along the way, however, people lost sight of the values of producing. It has become obvious what that does to the supply-and-demand relationship. As a society loses momentum in producing and increases its demands, prices rise, quality falls, and supplies grow short in relation to appetites. With each step forward in economic progress, people may generate new wants or demands. Scarcity is not an absolute; it is something people define for themselves. While scarcity may mean starvation to some, it may simply mean the lack of a second color TV set to others. Now Americans have to improve their supply and reconsider their demand. If they could grow as producers, they would not be so compelled to bury their regrets in consumption. The individual would increasingly ask "What can I contribute?" rather than "What can I get?"

The Most Important Kind of Growth

Henry Ford enabled his producers to be consumers. What we need today is for someone to enable consumers to be better producers—to abandon the notion of rapid, automatic, economic growth. Even leaders in the business sector warn that the old-style economic growth has outrun its course and must be replaced with new concepts of growth. Maurice F. Strong, an international entrepreneur, said at the 1979 Woodlands Conference on Sustainable Growth: "The 'new' growth approach must be based on the realization that the most important kind of growth is that which produces the maximum opportunites for self-expression and fulfillment on the part of individual people."

When people aren't treated as productive beings, they are less productive and more demanding than they could be or would like to be. Not merely is human growth desirable in itself; at this stage of industrialization, it is the only means for restoring vigor to the economy. Attention to individual human concerns can relieve some of the pressures that make for excessive demand and capitalize on some of the untapped resources that would improve the supply of high-quality goods and services.

It would be a "poor time for Americans to divide even further over the question of social values versus economic values," said W. S. Sneath, then chairman of Union Carbide Corporation, also speaking at the 1979 Woodlands conference. "Let us turn instead to finding ways for greater accommodation of both sets of values," he urged. "Social progress and economic efficiency are goals that we will achieve in tandem or not at all."

We are ready to begin a transition to a society where economic growth will be important but not as an end in itself nor as a cover-up for the lack of personal growth and satisfaction. Traditional economic notions, which have become so dominant in our thinking, have placed economic considerations above all others. We are beginning to realize, however, that what is good for humans is good for the economy. We are not in an either-or situation. People fulfilling higher levels of needs are the kind who will make the nation more productive in economic terms. Human productivity and economic productivity now go hand in hand.

What are these values that are rising in workers' hearts? The Public Agenda Foundation and the Aspen Institute for Humanistic Studies, in a major study called "Jobs in the 1980s and 1990s" reported: "These new values emphasize personal creativity, self-expression, adventure, the enjoyment of living for its own sake, the savoring of personal relationships, harmony with nature, the search for the sacred, and the satisfaction that comes with exploring the full richness of human experience."[3] These are the ingredients for a newer and stronger work ethic. In a 1982 survey of American workers, the Public Agenda Foundation found that among those who were more interested in self-development than in simply improving their standard of living more than seven-tenths endorse the strong form of work ethic—looking to work to satisfy inner needs—as compared to only half of the total population.[4]

The Producer Mentality

In short, the new quest is for intangibles. They are the sort of things people are more likely to pursue in the process of producing than in the consumption of what they produce. These are values which, although they threaten economic progress as we have known it, make people more work-oriented. If work organizations can respond to these new values and make self-development their new core project, there will be no need to choose between economic growth and improvement of the quality of life.

The person deriving psychic rewards from work is likely to be more productive than the worker carrying out the instructions of someone concerned only with the immediate economic results. In order to realize this potential, the workplace will have to be altered in work content, in the way work is packaged, and in organizational relationships to allow people to integrate their lives and enable them to share power and responsibility. People will become increasingly productive if the workplace offers them something to which they can commit.

The new values support a work ethic that is unlike the old Protestant ethic yet even more powerful in today's workplace. Under the old Protestant ethic the fruits of work were a sign that one might have been saved. The act of self-denial and willing toil was, in itself, seen as character building. But this was a misinterpretation of the Christian concept of "calling," historian-theologian Harvey Cox points out. It should summon man to "joy and gratitude" in anything he is doing—work or play.[5]

In a highly productive society, no one need be concerned with subsistence; even those who do not work are entitled to an income, Cox says. Unfortunately, he does what so many others have done; he assumes that we are in or close to a state of "Technopolis" in which machines do all the menial work. One problem with most utopian schemes is that nowhere have the conditions been attained that would support them on a broad scale; they have been tried only by a select few people living outside the mainstream economy. Another problem with these schemes is that they generally concern themselves primarily with man's hygiene needs. But people must have activities—work or play—through which they can meet their needs for esteem and self-actualization.

When we try to isolate work and play, we limit the potential rewards they can offer. The Puritans laid up a wall between them. We need, instead, a flux of work and play rather than rigid job structures with limits on what the jobholder must do and must not do. In their quest for wholeness, people suspect "there doesn't have to be a break between work and pleasure, between convictions and career, between personal ethics and 'business is business.' Fragmentation becomes increasingly intolerable."[6]

If, as so many futurists assume, we eventually reach a point where leisure time constitutes the major part of our day, a new work ethic based on self-development is likely to nurture the values and skills needed for meaningful leisure-time pursuits so that people will not have to seek escape in idle consumption. Also, if people are developing and fulfilling themselves at work, they are more likely to be willing to share the economic rewards with those who cannot or do not produce for one reason or another. If such sharing is something to which nonproducers are entitled, as Cox and others suggest, it is more likely to be seen as such by secure, fulfilled individuals. A producer mentality, therefore, can be more outward-oriented than the consumer mentality with its inherent selfish bias.

The calling to work that people are likely to hear today is unlike earlier callings that assigned them to given positions in the socioeconomic system. They now strive to be masters rather than slaves of economic forces. Even those who feel they are acting in obedience to God are likely to be interested in self-actualization as part of meeting God's intention for them. An organization can no longer count on people's abandoning themselves to robotlike work in a trade-off of their aspirations for economic suvival. Today's is a different kind of commitment, and it should not be confused with the duty-to-self attitudes that rendered so many people poor producers in recent decades.

A New Social Ethic?

Not everyone subscribed to the old Protestant ethic nor to the consumption ethic. However, at any time, one set of values tends to be the driving force of a society—the social ethic that brings individual and group goals into harmony. William H. Whyte's definition of *social ethic* in *The Organization Man* is a bit more cynical: "that contemporary body of thought which makes morally legitimate the pressures of society against the individual."[7] But Whyte, too, put the individual and society into balance when he asserted that individualism as stringent as that preached in the name of the Protestant ethic would not have been tolerated, and so is the complete denial of self called for in the social ethic that prevailed in the 1950s when he was writing.[8] The Protestant ethic was concerned with individual salvation, and the social ethic that troubled Whyte was concerned with improving society. For him, the organization man was the epitome of the individual surrendering to the group, acting under the spell of a powerful moral imperative.

In the 1950s, people accepted the system eagerly because they thought it was benevolent. However, they have seen since then that the system has gotten too big and has produced too many failures. During the 1960s and 1970s, self-gratification was preached as a moral imperative by those who shifted their strategy from being part of the system to getting what they could from it without pledging their allegiance to it. Although some of this thrust has been blunted by hard economic realities, we are not about to revert to the organizational imperative.

We now are on the threshold of an ethic that can serve both self and group. If (as we saw in the previous chapter) our new values center on a conserver society, ecological concerns, a new appreciation for nonscientific as well as scientific thinking, and commitment to something outside oneself, the drive for self-fulfillment could be turned into a producer-oriented, social ethic. For many, it might even become a moral imperative as the Protestant ethic and social ethic were. Both faded away because they were partial, uncompromising views of the truth about man. The Protestant ethic admonished the individual to work solemnly and restrained him from realizing his potential, but the new ethic will incorporate people's compulsion to grow. The social ethic led people to abandon themselves and their human relationships to the care of organizations, but the new ethic will be based on the belief that organizations are most effective when they are made up of self-reliant people who are developing as individuals and in their relations with others.

The Moral Dimension

This new ethic may or may not be a Protestant one or a Christian one. It is very much a Christian message that improvement of society begins with the individual, not the system; that improvement of the individual does not end with the self; and that man does not save himself through withdrawal from the world. It is in the material world that man can test himself and prove his faith and obedience. It is up to the church, therefore, to nurture the new ethic by teaching the loving and the patience people need in their process of *becoming*. It can show that work is love put into action. It can, especially, help people make that transcendental connection which can displace the awesomeness of living and dying.

Since this is a time of surging spirituality throughout the world, some people may make the new work ethic a moral imperative. When man works—especially when he approaches self-actualization—he asks, "For what purpose am I working?" Early industrial man, seeing himself in the role of provider for the family, won himself some self-respect—but not much. He did, at least, find an ethical justification for expecting nothing more from himself or for himself. In the future, we will have to allow for whatever spiritual dimensions the individual may insist upon. The new ethic should allow man to rise and lay claim to the spiritual world in which he seems determined to find a place. Adam left the Garden of Eden with head bowed to face a life of toil. Today, man is beginning to lift his head, not so much from a sense of pride in what he has done, but in search for what he must do. Seeing himself as a producer, he could work toward restoring the harmonies charged to him in Genesis: harmony with God, nature, fellow man, and self.

Economic imperatives are drawing attention to work and work organizations, but they will not be the sole determinant of future changes. Attributing only economic values to work has rendered it meaningless and less than a human endeavor for many. A person is most truly at work when he presses the limits of his abilities and grows, challenging himself and the universe. It is in working to satisfy his higher needs that he becomes truly man. He searches for significance, knowing that people are remembered for what they produce, not what they consume.

The degree to which the drive for self-fulfillment becomes a developmental one for the individual and society will depend heavily upon the encouragement, models, guidance, and resources provided in the workplace. What becomes of potentially positive and powerful attitudes toward work will depend on what the workplace demands of people and what it offers them.

If we no longer exclude personal growth and transcendental values from the workplace, we will also be able to bring the corporation out of its isolation from human problems. "The mainstream institutions of society also must accommodate the spiritual needs and hungers of people," says Maurice Strong. "This cannot simply be left to a few fringe institutions."[9]

PART II
THE CHANGING
WORKPLACE

8

The Corporation:
Positive and Infinite

A SHIFT IN THE WAY PEOPLE PERCEIVE THEMSELVES, a broad sweep of new values—all the factors needed for a new work ethic—are available. Yet, people need skills and opportunities to put their attitudes and beliefs into action. They need mechanisms through which they can do those things they want to do.

Whenever societies have undergone major change, they have been propelled by either existing or new institutions—a church, the educational sector, a political party. What institutions will Americans look to now? Which are best suited for nurturing the self-development ethic and making it a productive force? The old work ethic with which so many people are familiar was carried along with the thrust of Protestantism—through the churches whose influence affected nonmembers as well as members.

However, the church does not play a central part in Americans' lives today. The majority does not feel the hands-on guidance by the church. Furthermore, there is not a church but many churches— many denominations and many nonchurch religions active in the United States today. There is, therefore, no central message—no cohesive social gospel. Churches vary from one another and change from time to time in their attention to the world of work. We cannot look, therefore, at this time to the "church" to preach a gospel dealing with the self-development ethic or to nurture a producer mentality.

Our schools have been pressured not to engage in conveying

values but to teach only cognitive skills. We are concerned that
Johnny learns how to read but we don't ask what makes good reading. In a rush to provide a "relevant" education for career preparation, we have said, in effect, that we do not want the schools to study
the values issues and human struggles that make for a genuine education. Atheists and the Christian Right have fought as allies against the
schools' dealing with matters of ethics; both oppose the teaching of
courses in such things as values clarification and sex education.

The family, a traditional vehicle for nurturing values and teaching life skills, has been seriously weakened in modern America. Many
children are growing up in single-parent homes, sometimes switch-
ing from parent to parent. Even children in more conventional family
situations do not get full-time guidance as they are exposed to all sorts
of life-styles and values in real life and via television. Few are under
the caring guidance of the neighborhood or community. We have
come far from the Puritan community in which everyone helped
keep everyone else in line. Youth as well as adults enjoy—or suffer
from—anonymity. Living lives separate from those of their parents,
they need not worry that neighbors will report any misbehavior to
their parents. Strangers fear to raise a hand to take corrective
measures because the laws discourage intervention.

A sense of responsibility and a role in the work of the family or
community are not being conveyed to enough people through the traditional nurturing vehicles. Interest in self-gratification weakened
these institutions that might have been expected to lead people to
genuine self-fulfillment. At this point in the awakening of a self-development ethic, the opportunity to nuture and reinforce the appropriate values and to develop the skills to put these values into action is
most likely to occur in the workplace. It is here that people can see
quickly and directly the results of their behavior and test their
beliefs. It is here that they are most likely to find the facilities and
leadership to help them develop their talents and become productive
in terms that are meaningful not only to them but to others.

The Corporate Influence on Values

There is little doubt that the corporation does influence people's
values. Because of the rising influence of the corporation vis à vis
other institutions, its impact on human values will increase, and its influence will become increasingly positive. Is this wishful thinking? Is
this expecting the corporation to abandon its economic mission and

take up a role for which it is totally unsuited or perhaps even unauthorized?

Even if the leadership of a corporation is interested primarily in economic results, it will have to tend more to human resources and human values to attain those results than it has in the past. As the interconnected complexities of technology, economics, and society have mounted, the corporation has had to dig deeper to tap the knowledge and new ideas in more quarters—internal and external—to know what people's wants are and how to satisfy them more effectively and more efficiently. The companies that become people-oriented, therefore, do best economically. They are not wishy-washy, say Thomas Peters and Robert Waterman, who profiled companies widely regarded as excellent according to several financial and nonfinancial criteria in a study done by the consulting firm McKinsey & Company. In their best-selling 1982 book, *In Search of Excellence*, they reported that "companies whose only articulated goals were financial did not do nearly as well financially as companies that had broader sets of values."[1]

Although the corporation in a free market economy has demonstrated its superior ability to foster economic growth up to now, its impact on people's values has not been totally positive. It has succeeded by taking the limited economic view of people, but its future progress will depend on taking a broader view of man, seeing individuals' potential, and helping each member of the organization to reach toward that potential.

The social role of the corporation is the subject of long-standing debate, however. Some people, including those with considerable influence, see the corporate role in very simple terms. They assume the corporation is a direct descendent of the proprietorship and, therefore, bears only the responsibility for earning a profit for the owners. Others cast this role in a slightly more philosophical light, saying the corporation exists to provide goods and services for society.

The smallest corporations do represent little more than the means of livelihood for the principal investors—perhaps nothing more than a job. Nevertheless, from the hiring of its first employee, the corporation takes on new obligations. As its impact on people—employees, customers, suppliers, owners, the public—grows, the corporation becomes more and more a public entity. At some point, its effects as an intruder in the physical environment, as a taxpayer, as a user of public infrastructure, and in many other ways, including the shaping of the values of its various constituents, take it from the private into the public realm.

It becomes increasingly essential, then, that the corporation fit the prevailing value structure both in its products and services and in the means and manner in which it operates. In the future, the workplace will become a most appropriate place for resolving values issues so that the economic and noneconomic objectives established there will contribute to the sustainability of both the individual and the corporation. When people were concerned with economic survival in a preglobal economy, they permitted the corporation to be simply an economic instrument. As people now respond to higher levels of needs, however, the corporation must expand its scope to serve those needs.

Expanding the Corporate Purpose

By legal definition, a corporation is a limited-purpose, limited-liability "person" or entity. Still, most of us see the corporation as the sum of the people who own it and who work in it. We feel that these people are responsible to us in our various relationships to the corporation. It would be wrong to say that man is nothing more than the atoms which make up his body or that he is subject only to physical laws. It is just as wrong to say a corporation is nothing more than what is provided by law. The atoms of man are, in reality, energy; man is the sum of these energies and possibly more. Likewise, the corporation is energy; its potential power approaches the infinite.

When people deny that the corporation has social responsibilities, we should ask if that means the individual has no social responsibilities. People are people inside or outside the corporation. We don't compartmentalize despite what the law says. If we believe the individual has social responsibilities, we can logically conclude only that the corporation does, too. The good or the bad that comes from a corporation depends on the people within it. Some people have advanced proposals for legislating corporate social responsibility in one way or another; we might ask, "Why not also pass legislation ordering all individuals to be socially responsible?" If we want social responsibility from our corporations, we must nurture the feelings of such responsibility in the people who make up the corporation. If we permit people to see themselves only in economic dimensions, they will see their corporations only in economic dimensions.

For the corporation to become a meaningful social instrument, society must trust the corporation's intentions, and the corporation must want to play that role. Up to now, the corporation has been comfortable with the consumption ethic and its own limited economic role. Both the public and corporate management are coming to see the corporation as more than an economic instrument, however. The requests and demands that the public has laid against the corporation in recent years are highly visible. Management, likewise, is broadening its vision of what the corporate mission should be. Many executives believe the corporation is responsible to constituencies other than shareholders and that the large corporation is a political entity rather than a strictly economic one.

It is true that no "official" or legal mandate has been given the corporation to become a social instrument. It has no charter to engage in values issues, and corporate management has not been elected to do so. But neither individuals nor corporations "that guide their conduct by ethical or social values beyond the demands of law should be constrained merely because they are not elected to so do. The demands of moral responsibility are independent of the demands of political legitimacy and are in fact presupposed by them," say Kenneth Goodpaster and John Matthews, Jr., two Harvard Business School teachers of corporate responsibility and business ethics courses.[2]

Those who have pressed for the corporation to take up more social responsibility have all too often done so with single issues in mind. They have asked for official corporate action to right some wrong when neither the internal corporate climate nor the external one offered a consensus for such actions. Sometimes a responsibility has been pushed onto the corporation in an attempt to shift it from the individual to some third party. The best social action, however, is not the third-party type but one that involves committed individuals.

In 1982, President Reagan urged the business community to fill the gap created by reductions in government spending on domestic programs. Some business executives tried to rally others to increase their corporate giving and, especially, their lending of manpower to civic activities. The gap was far too big for business to fill, however. The unfortunate part of the situation was that attention was focused on filling the gap—a short-term measure—rather than on reducing it by eliminating some of the need for assistance. Not enough was said or done about the long-term potential of the corporation to help people grow so that they become productive in ways that would ease or fill many of their needs and lessen the demand for someone to do something for them.

Corporate social response is sometimes measured in terms of its charitable contributions, but far greater impact can come through the net positive effect of its products, the nature of its selling efforts and advertising, and its people-management methods. Businesses across the country have given far more in employees' time—either officially or through individual, voluntary efforts—to work on civic and governmental activities than they have in outright dollar donations.

Business contributes to the erosion of its own legitimacy when it insists that it has a single purpose and that is should not be involved in curing social ills. Owners and managers have done a great deal to confine the corporation to a limited economic objective. This has driven them into a head-to-head confrontation with workers, government, and the public since maximizing their own financial income means striving to minimize the return to others.

Greater corporate contribution to human growth will come, not from a sudden burst of nobility, but from recognition of the fact that the corporation is a process—an increasingly human process. It will not result from legislating what a corporation cannot do but from people's looking to themselves and to one another in organizations and saying "Here's what we *can* do." This is not to say that corporate leadership is totally lacking in nobility. In this age of criticism and skepticism, people overlook the positive impacts business has had on society: the creation of material wealth which has enabled people to turn their attention to the quality of life, the nurturing of technical and social skills in members of the corporation, and the many examples of ethical behavior being prescribed as a way of doing business.

Many managers in the top and middle ranks are convinced that the business corporation should lead in setting ethical standards for society. Moreover, they do not feel they are compromising their economic objectives in doing so. In the late nineteenth century, sociologist Emile Durkheim advocated that the occupational associations of that time reinforce morality since the family was becoming increasingly weak in that function.[3] Today, we may put the corporation in that same position. "Because the business of business is cultural as well as economic, the corporation has a responsibility for sustaining values," says Professor John Flaherty of Pace University. "In the final analysis, the corporation will have to justify itself not only in terms of economic performance but in the fashion it contributes to the quality of life. One dimension of this task is its compatibility with spiritual values." That would be a radical expansion of the corporation's mission, but Michael Novak, in *The Spirit of Democratic Capitalism*, insists: "Economic rationality . . . is not as merely instrumental or morally empty as some may think. The virtues it requires, and the virtues it nourishes, are indispensable to a self-governing polity and to a sound morality."[4]

Events of the 1970s and 1980s suggest that economic development has reached a stage at which economic objectives cannot be served unless human values are incorporated into the corporate processes. Otherwise, workers become less productive, management effectiveness is impaired as it works against its own conscience, and the public resists technological advances. Any economic growth or technological advances are justifiable only so long as they serve the long-term, global interests of humankind.

Although we once supported the corporation with values that contributed to the growth of economic power alone, we now find that our fundamental economic strengths put us into position to support noneconomic values, and our recently revealed economic weaknesses demand it. Even those managers and shareholders who are interested only in financial results cannot ignore the importance of the human factors. As the economic climate becomes more and more internationalized and complex in itself, the corporation must maximize the effectiveness of its human resources. Economic necessity, therefore, will be the flywheel that will maintain the momentum to fashion a new ethical base for the corporation.

Some people find it frightening to consider that the corporation might be the prime vehicle for nurturing human values in the foreseeable future. "It's a hell of a place to learn values," one manager told me although he admits that he believes there is a small but growing number of managers who could do a good job of shaping positive human values. Today, there are either more such managers around or more who are willing to come forth since they feel they have some support for venturing into that function. They believe the corporation cannot ignore the values issues in which it is immersed. Rather than being on the defensive and acting value-free, they would prefer to acknowledge the need for corporate involvement with values.

Facing the Values Issues

The workplace is not and should not be a place for sermons and worship, but it will increasingly have to deal with people's ethical, moral, and even spiritual dimension. It will be influenced by a worldview far larger than the strictly economic view that has so dominated it for centuries. If people are to work together effectively in an organization, they must have a set of shared beliefs. There must be certain values upon which they agree so they can establish trust and common purpose. The corporation need not preach morality, but it should act within people's moral expectations and, through its policies and procedures, convey some underlying moral position. It should not propagandize or proselytize, but, in its development of people, it can lead them through the tests of reality as to what makes for effective individualism, personal growth, and community action.

The corporation is not about to become a religious institution, but people working in American corporations may already be more "religious" than they realize. Their corporate actions are influenced, both directly and indirectly, by religious forces.[5] Although the number of people in workplaces is greater than that in places of worship, members of both traditional and nontraditional religious bodies do bring their values to the workplace.

The workplace is the place where people can be ushered into an appreciation of the new paradigm and acquire the skills for living fuller lives. It can nurture both individual and collective action. The many people who expect too little from themselves and their work can be introduced to the concept of self-development at work. As they acquire both technical skills and the ability to express themselves, they will move toward self-reliance and a healthy interdependence. As they see themselves and their organization progress and feel a sense of "ownership," they will acquire a sense of the future—a sense of becoming. These are the qualities the corporation is obliged to nurture if it is to be a viable entity in a changing world.

Although managers and nonmanagers alike may think the corporation can be or should be value-free, everything that is done in or by an organization plays some part in shaping the values of its members and the world outside. Leadership in a company—whether it is good or bad—is more influential than most other forces acting on people today. Strong corporate cultures provide the structure and standards for behavior.

When managers "talk down" to employees or treat them in ways that reflect a belief that people are irresponsible, they are likely to convince people that they are irresponsible. When they engage in favoritism, they encourage workers to become "politicians" rather than craftsmen since they signal that it's politics, not good work, that pays off. When advertising appeals to emotional logic, it causes people to make the wrong "connections"; these messages do not create a mentality that can deal with the precision and logic needed on the job. When companies rely on sex in advertising their products, they help

mold attitudes that place little value on responsibility and genuine fulfillment. But, just as it can shape an illogical, consumer mentality, the
corporation has the powers to foster a conserver–producer orientation for its own self-interest and for society's good.

Developing People

The corporation may choose to provide the setting in which people can develop an awareness of their own potential and a tolerance
and understanding of differing values—an important contribution
toward helping them live in an era of diverse values and beliefs. In the
years ahead, the workplace will become the arena where "social conflict generated by slow growth will be expressed, and where practical
solutions and a new social consensus might be forged." Society's attention will be focused on the workplace because "it is here that
many of the crucial issues of social stability, social justice, control
over inflation, and the health of the democratic process will be de-
cided."[6]

Beginning with the nurturing of self-respect among its members,
the corporation can lift people from a me-centered orientation. It can
build character as a by-product of people's being productive. Productivity, in turn, is a product of people's character; it is determined by
the quality of effort devoted to work activities and the quality of
results. It depends on the worker's caring about himself, the product,
fellow-workers, the person on the other side of the worker–manager
line, and the end user of the output of his efforts. It reflects attention
to effectiveness as well as to efficiency, contrary to popular notions
that productivity improvement is simply a matter of cost reduction.

A sense of order—one of man's essential needs—will come, not by
establishing more and more sophisticated systems and controls, but
through direct personal relationships and working out agreements,
face to face. Personal responsibility cannot be legislated or controlled, but it can be learned on the job as people see what they can do
for one another. Enlightenment, not regulation, leads people to create unity out of their diversity and cooperation out of their selfish interests.

The movement in recent years to forms of participative management, in which workers at all levels participate in appropriate problem-solving and decision-making activities, reflects the changing national culture. The workplace is being opened up to freedoms for the
worker that he traditionally had to surrender at the plant gate. The

corporation, in turn, will find its freedoms better supported by its own members. Workers' reluctance to do so, or their outright anti-corporate behavior, has been fostered by a tradition of conflict. After all, a culture in which people watch the minute hand for starting work, eating lunch, and going to the restroom is not a culture that will earn support for the owners of the clock.

Public Support

A primary reason for the loss of support for the corporation and the dimming of the sense of progress in America is the fear that corporations will advance technology without regard for the needs and concerns of people. There is no better insurance that the human hand controls "progress" in a high-technology society than to ensure that corporate leaders think first in human terms—that they recognize that the technologically better way or more efficient way may not be better for people. When the corporation elevates human growth and sees itself as an integral part of society, it will respond to a totally new array of reasons for being. Eric Trist, a founder of the Tavistock Institute of Human Relations in London, has said: "Traditional organizations serve only their own ends. They are, and indeed are supposed to be, selfish. The new paradigm imposes the additional task on them of aligning their own purposes with the purposes of the wider society and also with the purpose of their members."[7]

The corporation is the innovation arm of our society. As it develops and markets new technology, it both responds to and causes change in values. The American public seems to understand this. In a Lou Harris survey for Sentry Insurance Company, most respondents said they believe decisions about technology should be left to business. When asked who should play the most influential role in decisions about which innovations and new technologies are pursued, 54 percent answered "business." Only 26 percent said government should make such decisions, and only 16 percent would give primacy to consumer or environmental groups.[8]

The public looks to business to manage decisions about technology because that is largely where the people with the know-how are. This is where theory and practice come together and people know the good and the bad regarding any new development. It is, therefore, up to the corporation to make known to the public the costs, benefits, and risks of proceeding with or refraining from specific technological innovations. The corporation must help the public make evaluations and assign priorities to both economic and noneconomic objectives. It should not regard itself as the agent for carrying forward some technological imperative, extending technology to its fullest at every opportunity.

Values do not flow through the corporation on a one-way street. In fact, the corporation behaves more like a marketplace, allowing values to be exchanged as people strike a deal for relationships that permit certain jobs to be done. In a free market economy, the corporation depends on the diversity, creativity, and freedom within it in order to be adaptive and responsive to change. The more people-oriented a corporation is, the more relevant it becomes to society's needs and the more likely it is to capitalize on what people are willing to commit to.

Educational Failure

The human development role of the corporation will depend on what is happening in the greater society—what is being done elsewhere to nurture values and enable people to acquire skills to lead fulfilling lives. Unfortunately, many people coming to the workplace are ill-suited to perform the available jobs because they lack basic skills. Employers report that many of their secretaries cannot read adequately to perform their jobs, clerical workers cannot work with fractions, and too few managers can write grammatically correct letters. Fred T. Allen, chairman of Pitney Bowes, says his company has found that many job applicants with high school diplomas are "unable to adapt to the workplace and unable to handle basic tasks that involve reading, basic math, or other communication skills." Even worse, his company encounters job applicants who cannot fill out an application or answer questions during an employment interview. Rather than trying to lift the entire educational sector, Mr. Allen believes the corporation will have to "consider liberalizing our entry-level requirements for job-seekers, at the same time developing programs once they are employed to provide them with the tools to keep them on the job."[9]

Many firms are learning that if they want "better people," they will have to take motivated, intelligent candidates and train them in skills that can make them productive. They realize, too, that some people come to the workplace without the motivation required for learning. This poses a double problem but one that the business sector alone is likely to make a major contribution toward solving in the foreseeable future.

Americans have not fully appreciated the disparity between their education and that of other industrialized nations. We fall far short in language, communications, and computational skills and in the sciences. We cannot compete in a high-technology economy if people are not better educated than they are today. An uneducated individual cannot fully enjoy the fruits of such an economy, and the threshold for being "educated" is rising higher and higher. Even more frightening is the fact that a poorly educated populace renders a high technology society highly vulnerable to collapse.

In its earlier days, mass education in America concentrated on basic courses in reading, writing, and arithmetic. But, says Alvin Toffler, it had a "covert curriculum" which taught people "punctuality, obedience, and rote, repetitive work." It served to turn generation after generation of young people into "a pliable, regimented work force of the type required by electro-mechanical technology and the assembly line." [10]

Educators have moved away from that sort of manipulation and responded to people's clamor for credentials in the form of diplomas, degrees, or credits that will give them entry into jobs. They are responding to a job ethic, not a work ethic or producer ethic. Their attempts to make education relevant to existing jobs has reduced education to a job-readiness process that too often provides people with obsolescent skills or no skills at all. Training for job-readiness builds skills whose values may soon perish. People need a genuine education that gives them the tools for learning and adapting all through their lives.

"What America will require is workers who are humane individuals, with analytical and entrepreneurial skills, who know how to work in groups, and who know how to solve problems," says James O'Toole at the Center for Futures Research, University of Southern California. The "grunt work" that high schools and two-year colleges train people for will be done by machines in the future, he warns. These people, who may appear to be best prepared to find a place in the job market, are the ones who are most likely to be victims of change.

The schools should teach not only cognitive skills, they must help people prepare for a lifetime of work and leisure by nurturing self-discipline and instilling the desire to learn. For the jobs of today and tomorrow, we should feel no need to ask that the schools manipulate people with the old "covert curriculum." We need, instead, to help young people see the potential in themselves and sensitize them to the delicate balance between individual and group. They will need, not only problem-solving skills, but problem-finding skills. "In today's complex world, we've got to prepare our young people for a future where the choices to be faced can hardly be imagined now. It's essential that our great universities not only teach how to solve problems, but also how to participate with society in determining which problems ought to be solved," says Harry Gray, chairman and president of United Technologies.[11]

We cannot ask that the school truly educate and, at the same time, refrain from conveying values. The process of education itself is predicated on placing a positive value on knowledge. It presumes the student possesses certain valued traits such as the self-discipline needed in order to learn. An education that is useful for building character and opening the individual to personal growth leads to the study of what has been important to others, what has worked and not worked in the past. If people ignore values or treat all values as equal, they discard social and moral imperatives and deal only in personal taste, but a society cannot remain a society for long if it has only diversity of taste and no core of values to bind it together. This does not mean educators must propagandize or manipulate; a true education, in fact, creates a diversity of opinion, not sameness. An education free from dogma is the best route to meeting individuals' fulfillment ethic and the needs of the job market at the same time. The individual, business organizations, and the community at large are all served when the educational product is the development of character, self-esteem, and the drive for self-actualization.

Education: Business's Business

Unfortunately, the education sector is likely to wait for the business sector's lead before it brings all its forces to bear on this type of education. If business is to fill its human resource needs in the meantime, it will have to do an extensive education and training job. The business corporation will have to take up the primary responsibility for training newcomers to the workforce and those who are rising to more demanding jobs. It will also have to retrain those people who lose jobs through structural changes in the economy, helping them not only to acquire new technical skills, if needed, but to adapt to different industry cultures in which the manner of dress, the amount of discretion in the work, and the ways of relating to one another may be unlike those in the industry where they worked previously.

Since the educational system is not giving people rigorous enough preparation and since the economy is increasingly dependent on a higher level of knowledge-work, business has little choice but to step up its education effort. Business cannot expect to find a ready-made workforce, and so it will have to upgrade what it has. Actually, it does this with other resources. When it comes to making steel, for instance, management expects to extract iron ore from rock to begin the process and to undertake numerous steps of heating, cooling, blending, and forming. For some reason, however, when it comes to people resources, management too often expects to begin with a finished product.

United States business firms are not accustomed to spending heavily for education and training. Much of the training it does offer —even at management levels—has to do with corporate procedures, teaching people how to behave in the particular corporate culture. Too little training is available for people to improve the skills needed for their present jobs or for moving on to better jobs. But, with the emergence of a self-development ethic within many people, companies will have to provide learning opportunities in a lifelong process. In the future, corporate education will increasingly become a matter of giving individuals what they themselves determine their needs are and less and less the top-down indoctrination emphasized in the past.

Business will take a relatively small yet important part in the nation's educational effort by lending teachers and equipment to the education sector. In some cases, it will actually bring the educational process into its own facilities. Many firms now encourage their employees to pursue continuing education at local universities or two-year colleges to advance their knowledge in job-related courses. Some even make space available so instructors can come to the students at a company location. A few firms have begun to encourage their employees to pursue *any* continuing education, even if it does not relate to their present jobs because they believe in the importance of developing the whole person.

The business corporation has become a growing force in American culture. It could become an increasingly positive one if a number of misperceptions about its practices and outdated assumptions about its purposes were removed from the path of progress. Both management and the public need a newer and broader view of the corporation. The public tends to see business as it was many years ago, and many businessmen have failed to keep abreast of how much people have changed. As a result, their demands on and expectations of one another are sometimes unrealistic and work to their mutual harm. The corporation is readier to contribute to the community than is generally assumed, and the human resources are readier to make their contributions through the corporation than many managers expect.

Reductionist thinking that caused jobs to be narrowly defined and managerial roles to be economics-oriented have given the individual and the corporation little common cause. This sort of segmentation runs counter to the feelings of unity which are stirring within people. Both work and the organizations through which it is accomplished will gradually be redesigned to aid the search for unity. New forces—internal as well as external—are changing what the corporation does and how it does it. The sweep of new values will no longer support single-purpose people in single-purpose organizations. Contrary to legal definition and contrary to people's outdated assumptions, the corporation is a growing force in helping people raise their expectations of themselves and develop in all their dimensions. In turn, human growth will raise the limits of what the corporation can accomplish.

9

Humanization
and Participation

A QUIET REVOLUTION IS TAKING PLACE—not in the streets or on the campuses, but in the business corporation. As it progresses, more and
more employees are being freed from dulling work situations, and
companies are increasing their effectiveness.

The revolutionaries are not the "have-nots" battling the "haves."
They are not from the ranks of the downtrodden, but from upper
management. They recognize that people can do more and be more
than is generally expected of them in the workplace. This is a movement with few leaders and no ideology. Its simplicity baffles those
who would try to prove its lack of substance.

Throughout manufacturing, service industries, retailing, whole-
saling, construction, and even government operations, there is a
widespread movement to change the way decisions are made and
jobs are structured. Taking an optimistic view of people's potential,
management is pushing decision making down the line and encouraging an upward flow of fresh ideas.

Companies are giving new responsibilities and opportunities to
white-collar workers, blue-collar workers, and middle managers.
Cases are accumulating by the dozens to illustrate that when people
have something meaningful to commit to, they can help make their
organizations more effective economically, technologically, and in
human terms.

Leaders in these organizations believe that the work ethic is alive.

They recognize people's limitations, but they see vast potential for improving their output by allowing people to make greater inputs. They believe that solutions to the problem of poor work behavior have to begin with the organization, and many of them are making fundamental changes to meet the work ethic where it is.

The main thrust of industrialization for centuries has been to dehumanize work and fit people to time clocks and machines. Supporters of humanistic or participative approaches to management are convinced that further progress, technological and economic, will depend upon making fuller use of human resources. They are working to put jobs and people back together for two sets of reasons: (1) economic pressures to achieve higher productivity and product quality and (2) people's need to grow and find self-fulfillment.

This movement was detected in the 1970s by several watchers of the workplace. In 1975, Ted Mills, former television executive and then director of the National Quality of Work Center, said: "In the past three years, there has been a steady increase in U.S. managerial concentration on the human factor in the production of our goods and services." He noted that, "Unlike the superficial and fleeting fascination with the human relations movement of a decade ago, this one has every appearance of coming from a significant change in management philosophy."[1]

The interest in human resources is not simply a negative reaction or an attempt to quiet people's dissatisfactions. It is, rather, a positive effort to develop a major, neglected resource. Favorable results have been apparent for many years in a limited number of companies, demonstrating that organizations that show respect for workers and develop their human resources are generally also leaders in innovation and economic performance. For decades, however, the growing body of so-called management wisdom in this country ignored the lessons these companies could have provided.

A crack has appeared in the old fortress of hierarchical management. We have to open companies to change, to new ways of dealing with employees, said Tom Graham in the early 1980s when he was president and chief executive officer of Jones & Laughlin Steel Corporation.[2] One of the new breed of executives, he opened his company to change—a company in an industry that has been one of the more tradition-bound, hierarchical, and change-resistant.

The notion of developing human potential, nurturing positive values, and conveying life skills as part of the economic process would be empty theory if not for the growing body of evidence that companies can do so successfully. As recently as 1978, in writing about technology and society, I could only claim that the movement lay ahead. "Humanization of the job will progress for two seemingly different yet compatible reasons. It meets the needs of workers—to which a growing number of managers want to respond. It also may be the only means of maintaining or raising productivity levels in a humanizing society."[3] But there was little interest in productivity (which, a year or so later, became a buzzword in business) or in unleashing humanistic forms of management.

Since then, company after company has ventured into quality-of-worklife programs, quality circles, other efforts to involve workers in decision making, and various attempts to humanize the workplace. Some have responded to economic imperatives; others, to their own humanistic inclinations, or both. Some old-line companies have taken the humanistic approach to management for decades. The companies named by William Ouchi in his popular 1981 book *Theory Z* and by Tom Peters and Bob Waterman in their 1982 runaway best-seller *In Search of Excellence* included some relatively young, high-technology companies, but, by and large, the strong, innovative, successful companies they describe have been using the "new" style for many years. Both old and new companies are proving that we are not in an either-or situation where companies must choose between humanistic management or economic objectives. In fact, it seems, if management tries to serve only economic ends, people will fight them as they try to serve their own economic ends. If, on the other hand, a company does humanistic things just to give people a nice warm feeling, it may fail economically. Management has to attend to both sets of objectives.

Releasing Human Energy

Generation after generation of worker has felt acted upon; most employees have been a passive rather than an active part of the organization. But workers want to work better and smarter, to produce the best goods and services they can—not serve some unsatisfactory norm that management imposes on them. Many of them complain that the company expects too little from them in commitment and talent. This shortcoming has been troubling business for a long, long time. When he published the classic book *The Human Side of Enterprise* in 1960, Douglas McGregor charged: "In its present form [the corporation] is simply not an adequate means for meeting the future economic requirements of society. The fundamental difficulty is that we have not yet learned enough about organizing and managing the human resources of enterprise."[4] Frederick Herzberg was sounding a similar warning at that same time. Our institutions are not structured to fit the nature of man; industry is one of the principal despoilers of man's effort to achieve happiness, he said.[5] Many managers have heard of McGregor and Herzberg, and some have read their works, but the thinking of these two men is probably more appreciated now than ever before. Their ideas have become highly relevant as managers consider ways to alter the form or style of their organizations.

The human relations and organizational development efforts of the 1950s and 1960s were little more than a cover-up for Taylorism, which had dehumanized work by breaking down jobs into simple, repeatable tasks. They attempted to close the corporation–people gap by changing people's behavior and taming some of their dissatisfactions. The current movement to humanistic management is not just a response to a new breed of worker who is demanding certain rights or entitlements, but a means of tapping the potential of even those workers who never thought of asking to participate or to have their jobs enriched. Many workers have never even become aware of their own deep-seated need to participate in decisions affecting them or to make work a meaningful part of their lives. In some cases, they lack the expectations as well as the skills that would be required to play an active rather than a passive role in doing their day's work. Beneath their negative work behavior, which has harmed productivity and workmanship, lies the human ability to solve problems, adapt, and grow. Today, a growing number of leaders are working toward releasing that potential energy and splitting the atom of organizational mediocrity.

When companies encourage workers to participate in decision making, they do not intend that all workers be involved in all corporate decisions. However, they do open the process to workers at all levels, and thereby permit them to make decisions in areas about which they have direct information and are in the best position to study the situation. Hourly workers may order parts, manage their own budgets, plan their working hours, make suggestions when new equipment is being designed or installed, and even interview job applicants for their department. Sometimes "behind the scenes" workers deal directly with customers and suppliers and thereby get a feel for the impact of their performance on other people. Participation also permits workers to provide information and make suggestions on matters for which someone up the line will have the final decision-making responsibility.

At the outset, when this type of participative process is begun, management has to make it clear what the boundaries are on people's participation. Lower-echelon employees are not invited to participate at the highest policy levels of the corporation, and most aren't interested in doing that anyway. At higher levels, more managers are being permitted to shape corporate policy; sometimes policy is completely determined by a number of managers arriving at a consensus rather than by one person at the top.

It is likely, then, that the corporation will become more and more responsive to the values of all its members in setting its major policies and objectives as ideas, feelings, and values are brought into the open. As workers express themselves, the corporation is more likely to be in tune with the values of society. Gradually, the workforce will have a significant influence in harmonizing what the corporation does and how it conducts itself with the values of the greater society.

Fundamental Change for Managers

The concept of worker participation confronts many managers with the need for fundamental change in philosophy. For both managers and those who are managed, it leads to the redefinition of work and working relationships. It is especially threatening to the autocratic manager and creates high levels of anxiety in managers who want to embrace the new thinking but whose education, work experience, and incentives all point in the other direction. "Am I going to be out of a job?" the dedicated foreman asks. Worker participation will reduce the number of traditional managers needed but increase the need for *leaders.* Yet, the threatened supervisor or manager doesn't realize that and can't visualize any role for himself.

Participation means that managers must learn to share power rather than try to accumulate it. It calls for deeper insights and broader understanding of human needs than many managers have acquired in learning how to manage the old way. Nevertheless, it can make for a smarter organizations. Today, some executives are admitting more openly that they have no monopoly on good ideas. They find it makes better sense to invest in human resources and let those resources improve the organization. Cooperation brings far more favorable results than one manager can attain through tight controls on what people do, they believe. I have heard many managers admit that the people "out there" in the plant or office know how to do their jobs better than anyone. The trick is to win that knowhow. As one mill worker put it: "The workers out here know how to do their jobs better than they are, but you gotta get it out of them."

Participative management will not become standard operating procedure for all corporations in the near future, by any means. It may take a generation to become the predominant mode. Yet, the pace of organizational transformation is accelerating because it is reinforced by people's new image of themselves. In his book *Ten Thousand Working Days*, Robert Schrank said, rather pessimistically, "If we are to change our institutional arrangements from hierarchy to participation, particularly in our workplaces, we will need to look to transformations in ourselves as well."[6] We now have such a transformation taking place.

More than Paternalism

People who look at humanistic management from afar sometimes see it as nothing more than paternalism, but it is fundamentally different. Fred Herzberg has pointed out to me several times that he sees paternalism as merely humane, not humanistic. The paternal manager takes a kindly view of people and treats them in ways that minimize dissatisfaction and discomfort. In fact, industrial paternalism may have grown out of the doctrines of Calvin, which made the "elect" responsible for the welfare of their charges.[7] In more recent times, some managers have used a pseudopaternalism to minimize worker discontent in order to drown out the overtures made by unions trying to organize their employees.

Paternalism puts limits on people. Paternalistic managers let their people know they'll be taken care of in return for doing what they're told. The manager who takes this humane approach might break jobs down into simple tasks and remove the need for decision making so things will be simpler for the worker. The paternalistic company does things *for* people.

Participative–humanistic managers *enable* people to do more for themselves. They "grow" people rather than simply "maintaining" them. Humanistic managers put jobs back together; as a result, they provide a greater array of tasks and the opportunity for worker decision making even in the simpler job so that the worker will be challenged to grow and experience the satisfaction of learning and being recognized for doing so.

Human relations experts, earlier in this century, strived to get workers to comply with management's wishes and feel that they belonged to the organization. The more current "human resources" thinking truly regards people as resources and recognizes them as full members of the organization. At a cocktail party, a corporate vice president was describing his company's new participative management process. A listener, eager to show his appreciation, injected "and your people feel like they arc part of the company." The vice president corrected him: "They *are* part of the company, and they know it."

The importance of the worker's serving a "client"—long advocated by Herzberg—is often a central part of improving the job and winning the worker's commitment. By focusing on the user of his or her output—the client—a worker becomes more attentive to the quality of the product. Not every product is obviously of great social benefit, and not all workers can feel they are doing good for mankind, but a worker can take pride in serving specific persons—the next person in the production process, someone in another department, or the customer.

The worker who senses a relationship with the product and user of it is likely to perform better. Dr. Toshio Ito, manager of Mitsubishi Electric Corporation's research and development department, explained to a group of us American visitors that the corporation must consider the product–man relationship. Speaking in a philosophical tone, he described three ways to think of this relationship: (1) the function of the product, (2) the amount of human sacrifice involved in producing it, and (3) the price that will have to be paid to possess it. The product must be viewed as a system that relates to people, he stressed. Then we can be creative and consider all the alternatives for producing what is desirable in human terms. Dr. Ito's observations provide a beautiful overview of humanistic management. After decades of management science and behavioral science, the concept of humanistic management seems strikingly simple.

Herzberg's thinking ran counter to the scientific approach to management that was rising through the 1950s and 1960s. As he was rediscovered in the 1970s, some companies began taking his job enrichment concept "straight"; others incorporated his basic philosophy into their redesign of work and organizations. Herzberg has not joined the participative management movement, however, because he has seen too much participation just for the sake of participation. Early in the movement, there appeared a host of consultants ready to teach companies how to engage in team building. But feeling that one is a member of a team may do little to improve productivity, product quality, or the worker's sense of well-being. Many jobs do not depend on one's working as a member of a team. Each member in an organization does, however, need good working relationships with certain other people in the organization, and these relationships don't mean much unless the individual is able to do a competent job. Herzberg has insisted that, without the skills to do the job, feelings of team membership do nothing to improve the worker's quality of work or the satisfaction derived from it.[8] In fact, participation by people who are unskilled and unprepared is likely to increase their dissatisfaction.

Hard Humanism

To be successful, in both individual and corporate terms, a participative program must not only develop cooperative relationships but deal with the structure of the job and the quality of performance. Management must give workers the tools and skills that enable them to feel good about having done a good job and learning to do an even better one. It must also see that supplies, equipment, and procedures are all geared to enabling the worker to do a good job. This is *hard humanism.* Helping people develop themselves could be misinterpreted as coddling people. But coddling is not humanistic; it's paternalistic. Paternalism limits people. It says, in effect, "If you work for me, I'll take care of you. You're not too bright; I'm going to tell you what to do. You're not too resourceful; I'm going to pay you well, I'm going to take care of your family, I'm going to provide you bowling shirts." Hard humanism is tough. It means: "If you work for me, you're going to have to learn. You're going to have to meet the standards that we've agreed upon. We're going to have to sit down and solve problems together. I'm going to tell you when you do well, and I'm going to tell you when you screw up. You and I are going to share some problems and work on them together. We're going to win a few; we're going to lose a few."

Humanistic management doesn't let anyone off easy—neither the manager nor the managed. Implementation of any of the participative processes will quickly show how effectively a company has been managed—how effective management's speaking, writing, and listening skills are; how much people trust the company; how well workers are trained in job skills; and how well workers understand the significance of their individual jobs and the work going on around them. Without firmness, the manager would merely patronize people and shield them from life's realities. People need feedback—positive and negative—to know how they are performing so they can learn and grow.

Some well-intentioned imitators of humanistic management in

the late 1970s and early 1980s tried to give workers warm, fuzzy feelings. That approach did little to promote either human growth or hard-nosed business results. Some of the early programs, aimed at improving worker morale, fell short on both counts. They invited participation but provided too little in the way of training and information flow to enable workers to really improve their performance. Workers soon realized the shallowness of the programs. Worker satisfaction depends on being productive and knowing it. The person who works without feeling productive leaves work without a full measure of self-respect. The more a person contributes, the more likely he or she is likely to feel like an important part of the company and like someone connected to something significant.

The ill-fated programs were relatively easy to implement but difficult to sustain. Frequently, workers became unhappy because there was too little substance to the change, and management was disappointed because there were inadequate improvements in productivity and quality. McGregor had written of an earlier round of "soft" management, calling it a "superficial reaction" rather than a change in fundamental assumptions about people and about managing.[9] Today's movement does reflect a fundamental change in assumptions although some who have joined it do not see beyond the techniques to the basic philosophy that is required if the process is to work.

Building a Federation of Trust

Trust is a key plank in a humanistic or participative approach to organization—worker trust in the company and company trust that the individual can contribute to the well-being of the group. The president of one small company tried to implement quality circles in his plant, but they failed in just a few weeks. He asked me to talk with his middle managers and explore how the process might be resumed. I started by asking them what had gone wrong. "The people didn't trust the company," one stated without hesitating. "The workers didn't have any good ideas anyway," another quickly added. There it was in a nutshell. The assumptions were not right for success. A lot of groundwork has to be done in such a situation to build trust and to give workers the information and skills to be able to come forth with good ideas.

There are cases where participation has the support of top management, middle management, labor leaders, and the workers. There are far more cases, however, where one or more of these parties distrust the others. Even in programs that are progressing well, there is often some skepticism. There are doubts about just what to do next as progress comes in slow, careful steps.

When Rohm & Haas (Tennessee) Inc. wanted to update its 1940s vintage Knoxville plant to meet the needs of the 1980s, management knew that workers would be affected both in the number of jobs and the structure of their work. It looked like fifty or more jobs would eventually have to be eliminated, and the United Glass & Ceramic Workers wasn't interested in the company's offer to join in the redesign process. The company had pledged that there would be no layoffs due to job redesign—that the reduction in numbers would come primarily through attrition, but the union had little trust in management.

The company proceeded with its plant modernization plans and, eventually, the union joined in with the understanding that it would drop out any time it felt it was doing a disservice to its members. Local union president William Wilkins says the company kept presenting a "quality of worklife" concept and it seemed only right that the union take a guarded look at the idea. Being in on the process would help keep union members and officials better informed of what was happening, the union leadership figured. When a task force of equal numbers of union and company representatives began meeting to discuss technological improvements and job structures, labor and management sat on opposite sides of the table and spoke guardedly. As time went on, they began to get to know one another, and trust began to build.

A big deterrent to plant improvement had been the number of job classifications which seriously hampered productivity from management's point of view. Now, all the jobs in the plant have been redesigned, and workers have enrolled in self-regulating teams. The number of job classifications has been cut dramatically. In the Plexiglas inspection and finishing departments, for example, the number was trimmed from seventeen to two. And union president Wilkins learned that people want to take on a broader range of duties, to learn, and to do new things. People whom he expected to stay in their old jobs volunteered eagerly for the newly expanded jobs.

In September 1981, some 1600 business managers and labor leaders attended a meeting in Toronto on the quality of worklife. They shared story after story about people working toward improved quality of worklife, better decision making, and more effective organizations. These people were not dreamers. The stories of progress did not come from special cases in leading-edge industries or just from nonunion companies. Testimonies were offered by Bethlehem Steel Corporation, General Motors Corporation, the United Auto Workers, and the United Steelworkers—companies and unions whose traditions include some tough labor–management confrontations.

The success stories were not the kind that made listeners want to run out and "buy" a similar package. They revealed that every situation is different, that progress comes slowly, that trust can be built, and that all parties concerned must be willing to learn and adapt. Traveling under such banners as "quality of worklife," or "quality circles," or "involvement groups," these activities are pointed toward the day when both workers and management win.

The auto industry has launched numerous participative management efforts. In 1973, General Motors initiated its "Quality of Worklife" program on a voluntary basis. Operating managers who wanted to explore any concept for improving the quality of worklife in their organizations were encouraged to do so. They were not limited in what they could do. Later, all operating units were required to develop some sort of quality-of-worklife program. Again, each manager was free to choose his own approach.

The "program" is, therefore, not really a program. Management and union leadership at each unit decide what practices might meet local needs and interests. The objectives they set include such things as improving working conditions, reducing product reject rates, or raising the level of worker safety. Most of the units provide training in problem-solving, communications, group dynamics, and job-related skills. One of the first and most dramatic quality-of-worklife efforts was begun in Tarrytown, New York, in the early 1970s. Ten years later, one of the long-term employees there commented on the changes that had evolved: "We used to get together and talk about what we could do *to* GM. Now we talk about what we can do *with* GM."

Ford Motor Company did not commit to its "Employee Involvement" program until 1980. Within about three years, however, the quality improvement concept had been implemented at nearly all of the company's U.S. plants. The steel industry, heavily unionized like the auto industry, is also moving ahead with participative management efforts. The basic steel labor contract of 1980 authorized the establishment of "labor–management participation teams." As the concept was implemented in 1981, workers at Bethlehem Steel Corporation, Jones & Laughlin Steel Corporation, and National Steel Corporation volunteered for team membership faster than they could be absorbed into the infant programs. The real proof of popularity with the workers came during the following recession-battered year. Some workers were showing up at their plants for team meetings even though they had been laid off!

Finding the Right Corporate Culture

Quality circles, a specific form of participative management, have gained popularity throughout U.S. business. They are a highly visible process given prominence in Japan, although the concept originated in the United States. With Japan's notable success in productivity, product innovation, and marketing, many American managers have been looking to see what they can borrow—or borrow back. Again and again, the following question has been raised: "Are quality circles transferable to the U.S. with its different culture?" Yes and no. It depends on the organization that tries to employ them. It is not a matter of American culture but of the particular company's culture. The process won't work in Theory X organizations, but it can work in Theory Y organizations.

Some people doubt that quality circles are transferable becasue the United States does not have the homogeneous society that Japan has—what they perceive as a culture based on submission to the group. From this, they conclude that participative management in any form is not likely to work in the United States. What is the American situation? Americans are seeking interesting, challenging work; personal growth; integrated lives where work and nonwork activities reinforce one another; and something or someone to which to commit. The business corporation needs improved productivity, more innovation, improved quality, and the ability to adapt more readily to change. Both the worker and the manager should, then, welcome processes that are based on respecting the individual and provide opportunities for personal growth.

These new forms of management fit with McGregor's Theory Y organization, which assumes that people want to work, solve problems, and take responsibility for themselves. They respond to Herzberg's assertion that workers have to find something to love in the product or the work itself. They attend to Maslow's upper levels of need—belonging, esteem, and self-actualization. They match Daniel Yankelovich's concepts of seeking self-fulfillment and commitment.

These approaches to work require that management understand the inner nature of people and not let that be obscured by what they may see in everyday behavior. Worker behavior can be discouraging. A manager who is finally persuaded that the work ethic is alive and that he or she should try one of these new approaches is likely to be disappointed to find that people do not respond eagerly to a quick change in his or her management style. People have to be prepared for the change. They have to be informed about the new way of operating and be shown how it will benefit them as individuals.

Any would-be imitators of Japan had better note that the Japanese are not coddling people. They are genuinely using them as the nation's greatest resource. They look to their entire workforce for massive inputs of experience, expertise, and value judgment. The humanistic and participative management of Japan is not the result of its recent affluence and worldwide economic strength but a prime cause of it. The present style was deliberately set because that nation was in desperate economic straits after World War II. Kenichi Ohmae, Tokyo director of McKinsey & Company's consulting operations, says Japanese industry was shaped *after* the war, and the early postwar companies were like communes. Participation and a feeling of community were the building blocks.[10]

Part of Japan's competitive advantage is the special relationship among industry, the financial sector, and government. Japanese industry is able to afford modern equipment and operate at a level of profit that American firms would consider inadequate to attract investors. Even so, if American managers could deal with the "soft" factors as well as their Japanese counterparts, they could work some miracles with their existing plants and do a smarter job of building the plants of the future.

Worker creativity can sometimes eliminate the need for new machines or a new plant. At the Kubota Ltd. tractor factory in Osaka, I noted a hand-printed sign in front of a line of old grinding machines. I asked my host what the sign said. It had been put there by the quality circle working in that area, he explained, and it stated that the changeover time to switch from grinding one line of parts to another had been reduced to five minutes. "How much time did it take before?" I asked. "Two hours," he smiled.

The United States is different from Japan, but there is nothing about American culture or American companies that would justify the assumption that all the wisdom or creativity has been bestowed on some small fraction of people who happen to be at the top. Kenichi Ohmae, having consulted companies around the free world, observes that "the most successful large corporations today, regardless of nationality or industry, display a number of common characteristics.

They offer job security, tenure-based promotion, and internal development of people instead of massive recruiting campaigns. They provide endless opportunities for employee participation. They regard their people as members, not mere employees. They promote a common values system."[11]

William Ouchi, in *Theory Z*, also pointed out that some of the biggest and best U.S. companies like Hewlett-Packard, IBM, Procter and Gamble, Cummins Engine, and Eastman Kodak possess the same traits as the Japanese model. These companies did not take their present shape by copying the Japanese, however. They evolved in a natural adaptation to U.S. conditions.[12] Making the American corporation more democratic and "human" is a natural outgrowth of the American tradition of freedom and participation. We are free outside the plant gates and the office building; why not inside?

Many people have become accustomed to hierarchy. They feel they need to be told precisely what to do. Many are not in the right frame of mind for participation and involvement. In fact, the prospect can be downright frightening, especially if you lack the skills for dealing with others, for prioritizing problems, and solving problems in new ways. Despite the resistance that might be expected, however, workers have demonstrated an eagerness to join in well-intentioned, well-structured programs or processes. In cases where employees have been told about their company's intention to install quality circles and explained some of the fundamentals and benefits, for example, 90 percent typically say they want to try it. The circles of eight to ten persons, who do related work, meet weekly to define problems or opportunities for improvement in their area of operations, gather the pertinent facts, and develop a course of action. All this is new for many workers and will amount to nothing if the company does not provide training in problem solving, information gathering and analysis, and in functioning effectively within a group.

Changes in Management Readiness

Although quality circles spread slowly in the United States during the 1970s, the movement did not really catch on until management began considering some fundamental changes in its own behavior. The slow buildup was due not to the nature of American workers or American culture, but to management's posture.

Management's principal motive for implementing quality circles is generally the hope of attaining productivity improvement. Often, however, it may be primarily interested in improving the quality of its product or service. There are some purists who believe that quality must be the prime thrust. They don't rule out productivity improvement, however. They view it as a by-product of better quality because reduced scrap rates, less reworking of faulty products, and less follow-up repair in the field are directly related to productivity.

The success of quality circles or any other form of participative management need not be confined to the primary focus, however, and it seldom is. Although an organization can attain all the potential benefits simultaneously, any one of the improvements—in productivity, quality, or the overall effectiveness of the organization—might justify implementing one of these processes. The benefits are sufficient that some companies have moved deeply into training in order to improve workers' job-related skills, interpersonal skills, and understanding of company economics. If employees are going to make decisions and solve problems, they need a continuous flow of information on what the company intends to do and how it is doing. They must understand corporate objectives if they are to make them part of their own personal objectives. Some companies also take their employees on tours of customers' facilities to see how the products of their labor are being used and to learn what is important to the customer.

Training and information sharing determine whether the process is more than a fad. Investment in training has no end because the whole process depends on establishing a learning environment for management and nonmanagement personnel. The more sophisticated employees become as they work on productivity and quality matters, the more they demand information and know-how—generally far more than management is used to providing. This rising challenge to management is offset by the decline in minor complaints. Once people take on the problem-solving mentality and feel involved as part of the solution, many of their minor irritations no longer really bother them or are quickly resolved. "Once you get the 'ownership' of a problem at the proper level, the problem seems to disappear," says one plant manager; that frees supervisors to do more constructive work. "They can spend time on the front end, trying to figure out the right solution, rather than having to follow up to be sure people do things as they were told."

The quality circle concept is one of the most popular and most structured of the participative schemes. The structure, however, has to be based on a positive view of people or it is of little value. Practitioners warn management that the process is not something you do to employees, but something you do to yourself. Because the concept, if implemented, has the power to transform organizations, management must know that it wants to change, how it wants to change, and if it is ready to change. The big question is not "Are workers ready?" but "Is management ready?"

Management, hoping to get a quick payoff from ideas for cost reduction or quality improvement, may jump into employee participation too quickly and not make a long-term commitment to the process. It may not realize that participation depends on a change from traditional corporate culture to begin with and can lead to more and more change in the future. Although the quality-circle approach, for example, is designed to fit into traditional corporate settings without too much disruption, a company that has employed it for several years may find that the corporation eventually has to evolve to some new form.

Companies that are not pressured by competitive conditions may get by without participative management, but even they may eventually feel the impact of the movement. They could become vulnerable to a flow of workers to companies that have more positive corporate cultures and invest in the development of their human resources. Even in the weak job market of the early 1980s, more than one young jobseeker said he or she was looking for a "good company" to work for. The ones they had in mind were those that offer challenging work, a chance for continuing education, and room to grow. The new values are taking root, and they influence what people look for in their work. The most desirable employees are going to be attracted to companies that they perceive as being good for them.

When the double-barreled recessions of the early 1980s struck, more than a few people thought humanistic and participative management practices would be put on the back burner until companies had the time and resources to proceed. They were seeing these practices only as an effort to coddle people—a frosting on the cake. They didn't see that many managers were breaking from the approach usually taken in employee relations during tough economic times. All too often in the past, when business activity was depressed, a manager could assume, "If people want their jobs, they'll do as they're told." This time, managers with their backs to the wall were more likely to say, "Find any way you can to tap the talents of our people to get them to work together and help us do better." They did not resort to the usual "stick" to get people to work harder. They hoped to get people to work smarter by showing them their "stake" in the company's well-being. The corporation, therefore, is being kicked wide open as top management reaches down for help from anyone who will respond.

Some managers who had just begun to operate in a humanistic, participative manner were deeply troubled because their companies' desperate circumstances due to the recession forced them to lay off employees. They felt they were betraying the very people they had been trying to develop. Even in less pressed companies this was not a good time to test how well these programs could contribute to business growth. Limited budgets sometimes handicapped managers in providing all the training and assistance required for full success. It was also difficult to measure the short-term payoffs accurately since business activity was so depressed.

The net effect of hard economic times, however, was to spur the movement rather than kill it. More and more managers were willing to bet on the long-term or immeasurable benefits. Employee participation was growing fast because more and more people were convinced the American economic malaise was due to many years of inattention to the human resource factors. The greatest potential danger to the movement is its own success. The manager who observes success in another company might try to copy the techniques—buy the package—while holding to his negative view of people and nursing his distrust. His venture into participative management stands a good chance of raising worker expectations, failing to deliver improvements, and result in a worse situation than he had at the outset.

Worker participation undoes some of the controls that management has placed on workers—things that interfere with the natural process of people trying to improve the quality of their contribution. It means management has to accept people as they are rather than seek ways to change their behavior through systems or controls. Managers who take this approach realize there is a small fraction of any group who will not cooperate or contribute, but they do not let that minority determine the culture of the organization. They will dig deep to find the explanation for an individual's negative behavior. James Renier, vice chairman of Honeywell Inc., points out that managers generally don't ask the right questions; they are concerned only with what they see on the surface of things. Take the case of a worker who habitually rushes from the factory a little before quitting time and seems to lack a work ethic. She may live a long distance from her work—which means getting up at 4:30 A.M. in order to drop her children off at a day-care center and get to work by 7 A.M. Then, he says, a foreman who hasn't planned the workweek well asks her to work overtime. She objects because she is worried about her children. "We miss the point about the work ethic by not knowing the individual's objectives. Unfortunately, we ask 'What's the bottom line?' rather than 'How far do you drive to work?'"

Threatening the People
in the Middle

The spread of participative management practices will be limited primarily by the resistance of middle managers and first-line supervisors. These people perceive their jobs as being jeopardized. After all, they have invested years to win the right to make decisions. They feel they are the people who should know what to do and how to do it. Their knowledge and seniority have traditionally entitled them to power. Participation by their employees means that they have to share that power. When workers become involved in defining and solving problems, they will need data on costs, production schedules, pricing, and other matters as well as information about company objectives and performance. Managers and supervisors have traditionally resisted sharing such information because of company policy as well as their own personal inclinations.

Managers have to be convinced that, while their role as boss is ending, they will still have jobs if they operate as facilitators, helping others do their jobs. There will still be a need for people with leadership ability and for resource persons with special knowledge. Upper management has to help the manager or supervisor envision this new role. It also has to provide special training in interpersonal skills for the manager who will no longer be able to rely on the power of his or her position. Most importantly, recognition and reward systems have to be changed to convince the manager that his human resource development efforts are part of the job and that is what he is being paid for.

Union resistance to participation is not so strong as one might expect. Labor officials have not been the leaders in the movement, but they are slowly joining its ranks. When I noted in one foundry that jobs had been fairly broadly defined and the maze of job classifications that I would have expected there did not exist, I asked the plant manager if the company and the union had negotiated a streamlined list of classifications. "No," he said, but many work rules had been changed on the shop floor without formal negotiations. "The union leadership knows about it but won't write them into the contract. It's a union political matter."

Even for their own political interests, labor leaders are coming to realize that, just as unions once won respect for workers as economic entities, they now have to meet people's demands to be recognized as people. Some of them see unions threatened with extinction unless they catch up with workers and managers in the new philosophy. A few see the changes as a natural progression for the labor movement. Irving Bluestone said at the 1981 Toronto meeting on quality of work-life that achievement of human dignity is at the heart of the quality of worklife movement. "And that's what unions stand for. This is the natural culmination of the labor movement toward a better life."

Jerome Rosow, president of the Work in America Institute, has observed that "as management confidence grows and the partnership flourishes, the level of secrecy declines . . . shop floor leaders change their role from full-time grievance processors . . . and instead become active participants in problem solving. Major labor disputes, work stoppages, slowdowns, and wildcat strikes drop sharply; in fact, in many of the more successful programs they virtually disappear."[13]

Industrial Democracy American-Style

Participative management has developed spontaneously in the United States. It has not depended on legislation and bears little resemblance to the "industrial democracy" practiced in certain European nations. In fact, it makes no promises to let workers run or own the company. The American style is participation at the appropriate level. Although labor and management are adversaries at the bargaining table, both sides find they have plenty of common ground for cooperation between bargaining sessions. Foreign managers familiar with U.S. workplaces are, in general, impressed by the significantly less pronounced distinction between labor and management in the United States than they find in other nations—even Germany with its well-established industrial democracy. In the United States, the boss and the employee may well bowl, fish, or drink together. They are on a first-name basis. In other countries, I have usually detected a certain class differentiation—an unofficial but lingering separation of worker and manager; some U.S. managers refer to this gap in even stronger terms—a "caste system."

In some countries, notably Germany and Sweden, labor has attained "codetermination" through the political route. Neither labor nor management are especially happy with it, however. Labor thinks the concept has not been taken far enough; management fears it has gone too far. In Germany, beginning with the iron and steel industry in 1951, worker representation on the supervisory board of corporations has been provided for by law. Since 1976, German firms with over 2000 employees have one-half the board positions filled by representatives of labor; firms of 500 to 2000 reserve one-third of the board seats for labor representatives.

Even with these provisions, workers don't really have parity with management, and the flow of information to workers is not as good as that in many U.S. firms. Worker-directors become neither labor nor management. A Swedish manager says many of his employees are angry because their representatives withhold corporate information from them in order to satisfy their own need for power. Codetermination, at best, has served as a system of checks and balances rather than true cooperation or joint management.

The election of UAW president Douglas Frazier to the Chrysler Corporation board of directors did not stir much union interest in making that a common practice in this country. Workplaces reflect the societies in which they exist. Americans are less political than people of most, if not all, other industrialized nations. They have chosen not to politicize the worker–manager relationship by forming a labor party as the workers did in Britain or to fight for a German-type codetermination. They do make a distinction between labor and management for bargaining purposes because they prefer dealing as adversaries within the system to opposing the system itself.

American unions' primary interest in participation at this time is for workers to have a say in the situations that affect them directly; they are not interested in taking on all the troubles of managing the company. They and the company can benefit if they are privy to more corporate information, but they can obtain that without managing or owning the company.

Ownership of Oneself

Activists and writers frequently call for getting ownership of the corporation into the hands of employees in one way or another. While there may be certain mutual benefits in that, and while some companies do have methods for transferring some shares to the workers, employee ownership is no assurance that the corporation will be more humanistic in its dealing with employees or more socially responsible. Some management structure is needed even in a totally employee-owned company; despite a change of faces in the hierarchy, the questions of ethics, style, and culture may remain unresolved.

ESOPs—employee stock ownership plans—have been pushed by a few as the panacea for problems of productivity and morale. Company allocations of shares to employees represent financial gain for the employee and a bit of ownership, but they do not deal with the problems rooted in work content or in corporate culture and values. The share of corporate earnings that come through such mechanisms are tiny compared to the jobholder's basic wages or salary—too small to create a feeling of really being a part of the company, especially if everything else that made the job and the relationship undesirable remains unchanged.

Generally, these programs have been aimed primarily at providing some additional economic return to employees, thereby making them feel they belong. Nevertheless, they have not, in themselves, dealt with the development of people or the creation of meaningful work. In fact, they are sometimes a trade-off for putting up with meaningless work. Companies that concentrate their human resources strategy on financial mechanisms are dealing on the *humane* level; they are not meeting people at their higher levels of need. Because they concentrate on workers as wage earners rather than tapping the full range of work motivation, these programs cannot even give good assurance of job security.

Growing, learning workers are improving their own job security. For example, a team of diemakers at Ford Motor Company's engine plant in Cleveland told me they were bidding on jobs formerly done by outside vendors. As they had searched their area for problems to solve, they found more and more jobs that could be done internally. At a time when the company was making heavy layoffs in other departments, this group was expanding its number of positions.

Devices such as ESOPs or codetermination do not ensure that the company will be better managed or that employees will work smarter. Neither employee ownership nor representation on the board of directors will protect a company with old facilities, poor location, shrinking markets, or technologically obsolescent products. Winning employee commitment and greater productivity does not relate directly to the amount of pay and pensions the company can afford to shower on people. On the other hand, there is no reason why a genuinely humanistic management approach will not also provide good economic compensation. In fact, it usually does since the mutual worker–company commitment produces improved economic results which the company can share with employees. The worker thus gains economic as well as intangible benefits.

A worker who feels he or she is alive and growing on the job is more likely to feel like an owner of the company than the underutilized worker with a share of stock. People want to make a contribution, to do something worthwhile, to be part of something significant. They are not so concerned with owning a small share of the company as with owning 100 percent of themselves and the jobs into which they have invested sweat. A person needs to know that on any day, he or she might be a winner at work without waiting for an annual awards dinner or yearend bonus. At any time, as he finishes a task or assignment, wants feedback on a job well done—or not well done. (After all, there is no winning without some losing.) Too often, workers have been left to feel that there is no winning or losing, that they simply have to be there.

Business can no longer afford to pay people primarily for their physical presence. It needs their creative inputs to decision making and their commitment to implementation of plans. Managers, therefore, will need the courage to refrain from rigidly defining people's jobs and, instead, permit access to information and greater opportunity for exchanging ideas. They will increasingly be trying to learn how they can convey more information so workers can make smarter decisions about the aspects of the business that directly relate to them. This will not be easy because it runs counter to the traditional practice of giving workers as little information as possible—even withholding information that competitors already have. But in acquiring a fuller understanding of the company's financial situation, workers are more likely to appreciate the hard realities and work toward improving revenues and reducing costs. They are, therefore, less likely to feel compelled to make unreasonable wage demands to compensate for not being allowed to come alive at work.

The corporation can increase its effectiveness by seeing that information flows up, down, and sideways. Many companies, however, are suffering because they have prevented such flows. They have restricted strategy setting and planning to a few key people—people who, like any humans, couldn't possibly have all the information and insights they need to plan well and who couldn't have all the power they need to execute those plans. "The smart people were so smart that they had to spell out every detail of the corporation's strategy for three to five years," says Kenichi Ohmae. "Thus the dumb people never got the big picture."[14]

Since the "dumb" people don't know what the company's objectives are, they can hardly be expected to commit to them. In fact, the "dumb" people sometimes set objectives that are counterproductive. They prove to themselves how smart they really are by fouling up the product, their equipment, or the bookkeeping. They may even resort to theft or sabotage as a test of intelligence and influence. The "dumb" middle manager knows how little he needs to accomplish and still keep his job. His subordinates, in turn, know what their minimum performance has to be. This leaves the "smart" people commanding organizations made up of underachieving people.

There is plenty of evidence that when management shows respect for employees and responds to their desire for greater responsibility, achievement, and a say in decision making, they get commitment and creativity in return. That's good not only for the individual but for the company because creativity and commitment are what a business organization runs on.

New Technologies in Human Hands

People will embrace innovation and new technology if they are part of an open-ended, creative, learning environment which they feel they have a hand in shaping. On the other hand, managers and nonmanagers will resist innovation in order to protect narrowly defined jobs. When people believe they are part of the company, they welcome new technology which can help them do a better job. They may even suggest improvements that eliminate the need for acquiring new equipment. Some new plants are being built today with the people factors and new forms of company organization given the first consideration. To an increasing degree, companies are inviting blue-collar inputs into machine design, machine location, and plant layout.

In the late 1970s and early 1980s, Jones & Laughlin Steel Corporation opened eyes in that industry when its efforts in employee communications, education, and involvement resulted in bringing old facilities up to substantially higher levels of output with relatively little new equipment. Here was proof that the "hard" and "soft" factors of production are very much interrelated. It is no coincidence that the young, high-technology companies like Hewlett-Packard and Tandem Computers Inc. are also humanistic and participative. Creativity is a function of people. The development of new technology and the implementation of it depend, more than anything else, on the workforce—its attitudes, skills, motivation, and the chance to invest its talents. Creativity in the lab, in the plant, or on the sales call depends on people having self-esteem and commitment.

Technology was once managed best through massive hierarchical organizations designed to control processes and people. But that line of progress cannot be projected into the future. Organizations must innovate their structures in order to attain a greater ability to innovate. Ironically, the management of technology is becoming more and more dependent on the human hand in both its delivery and its acceptance.

American industry needs better technology in its plants and in its products. More importantly, it needs to make better use of the technology it already has. Although the Japanese have some advanced manufacturing equipment in some of their plants, they are, by and large, not a generation ahead of the United States. They are not using better equipment so much as they are using equipment better. Their marketing and manufacturing strength is not the result of superhuman top management, or superhuman middle management, or superhuman engineers, but the result of a super job of getting everyone involved in constant change and improvement.

Technology is creating opportunities for people to make a greater contribution. Although is is often regarded as inherently dehumanizing, it can be "a powerful medium for human connection."[15] Computers and communications systems give more and more people access to more and more information and to one another. The human and technological processes reinforce one another if people are permitted to participate in problem solving and decision making. Some of the hardware and software now available enable companies and individuals to be more humanistic. Even the bank teller who doesn't really know me can be a bit more personal, thanks to the computer, I found on one occasion; after I handed her my ID card in order to cash a check, she punched her keyboard and then looked up with a grin. "Happy birthday," she said. The data bank had told her the date of my birth. But it was her connecting it with that day's date and having the interest in going an extra step that personalized the transaction. The tools for exchanging ideas have never been more plentiful.

The worker is coming to see himself or herself as more than a wage earner and the company as more than a source of financial compensation. As both the worker and corporation become more dynamic and unlimited, they move toward what McGregor called "integration"—a situation in which members best achieve their own goals by serving those of the organization.[16]

The participation movement has already gone far enough to convince us that it could make the workplace the major vehicle to move the individual toward self-fulfillment. In the future, individuals will gravitate to the companies that permit them to be all that they can be.

Their creative performances and contributions will, in turn, encourage more and more managers to support the movement.

This could be the beginning of the end of industrialization as we have known it. It could be a greater step in the evolution of industrialization than were the abandonment of child labor practices or the 70-hour week. It could eliminate many of the dehumanizing aspects of industrial life such as standardization, specialization, synchronization, and centralization listed by Alvin Toffler in *The Third Wave*.[17]

Industrialization, which for so long alienated people from themselves, their families, their fellow workers, and their managers, is now beginning to help people integrate their lives. It once changed the image of man, but that image is changing again and will now reshape industrialization. As organizations become humanized, they will lift people to levels of accomplishment never attained before and on a wider scale than people have dreamed of during or before the industrial era.

10

Coming Alive at Work

A QUIET, PASSIVE, BANK EMPLOYEE HAS BEGUN TO ASSERT HERSELF in meetings, expressing good ideas for improving the operation of her department.

A divorcee, depressed for months since her marriage ended, sparks during a leadership training course. Her work has now become her "life raft."

A task-oriented worker, perhaps a bit of a workaholic, gradually comes to see the value of other people's ideas and of working in a group.

A company trainer who teaches fellow workers how to analyze problems and brainstorm solutions applies his skills to his volunteer fire department. The group develops ways to raise far more funds for fire-fighting equipment than ever before.

What's going on?

People are coming alive at work. This has happened in the past, but now it is happening to more and more people and to the types of people in the kinds of jobs where it was not common before. They are finding something of value in their work that makes their work more important to them or helps them in their personal lives. These examples of people finding "new life" are not the result of their managers' engaging in some sort of therapy program; they are the by-product of people's being given the opportunity and the skills to tend to business —to take some measure of control over their work situation.

More and more jobs enable people to engage in problem-solving with others. They are in a real business situation and they are solving real problems. They need to dig deep into themselves and listen intently to what others are saying if they want to come up with solutions that will make them successful. They are putting themselves on the line, and someone cares about how well they perform. When success does come, the person has something to feel good about. And along the way, he or she is learning new skills—something else to feel good about.

"Think for a moment about times in your worklife when you felt 'turned on' or excited about what you were doing," suggests Bob Ramsey, senior consultant for training and development at the North American Consumer Product Companies of Kimberly-Clark Corporation. Some of the things that give you a good feeling and motivate you, he says, include deriving a sense of self-importance from the work setting, being understood and accepted, achieving personal and group goals, having done quality work, contributing to the success of others, and being recognized for a job well done.

More and more people working in humanistic, participative situations are integrating their work and nonwork lives. They are seeing the relationship of their individual contribution to corporate success and the rewards that are coming back to them. They feel a sense of belonging and self-esteem that they can carry home from the job. They are learning what makes an organization work well and what doesn't. They are learning skills that give them the power to look more confidently to the future and feel that they can take a hand in shaping it.

At The Higbee Company, the Cleveland-based department store chain, sales personnel at all levels are involved in what the company calls simply "the process." It is a system that encourages individuals to act in an entrepreneurial mode by suggesting ways to improve customer service, reduce costs, and boost sales volume. One day, employees at one store scurried about wearing wildly-decorated tennis shoes—their agreed-upon way of boosting spirits in the face of the chores that normally go with inventory day. At times, customers may hear something like "WS-85" over the public address system; it's the store manager's way of letting employees know that they have hit 85 percent of their sales goal for the day. These are not gimmicks to keep employees entertained. They represent a dedicated effort to "use the knowledge of intelligent, alert, enthusiastic rank and file people to help manage the company and produce better profits," says Herbert E. Strawbridge, chairman of the company. As communications lines

open up, people see that many things can be done at their level to improve the entire company's performance, says Theodore Johnson,
vice president–personnel. "Management is creating an environment
where employees can do what they already know needs to be done,"
he adds.

Employees are permitted to work as though they were private
contractors at Crown Zellerbach Corporation's logging operations.
As a result of a five-year agreement made with the International
Woodworkers of America in 1982, workers plan their own work
schedules and time off so long as they meet production goals. Operations are run by committees of management and union members who
resolve pricing and pay issues; promote productivity; identify training needs; and review data on production, safety, and quality.

At Hoffmann–La Roche Inc., more than fifty secretaries were "in
on" the major acquisition of word-processing equipment. Since they
were to be the primary users of the equipment, management figured
they were best qualified to express their needs and evaluate the capabilities of various lines of hardware and software. The secretaries
visited IBM, Xerox, Exxon, and other producers of word processors.
One important consideration that came out during this evaluation
was the fact that whatever was purchased would have to span the
needs that differed from one department to another. Perhaps the
most important benefit to the company was the subsequent support
of this corps of secretaries who were determined to make the system
work.

Humanistic management's success has been well-documented
from the company standpoint, but little has been written yet about
the personal success stories—about individuals coming alive in their
jobs as a result of it. We should not be starry-eyed in expecting new
processes and structures to be put in place overnight so that everyone will suddenly blossom at work, however. A long maturing and
learning process lies ahead of us. Yet, the process has begun, and it is
exciting to watch.

Although we have been hearing more and more about corporate
efforts in human resource development in recent years, we may miss
the essential truth about what is happening: Individuals are awakening to the possibility of personal growth and finding opportunities to
attain it. The team building we hear about is secondary to the development of the individual. The skills and values a person acquires on
the job can make him or her a stronger individual and, at the same
time, a stronger member of the community. As jobs are enlarged,
enriched, and "unpackaged," the worker is gaining far more than the

opportunity to be effective from the company viewpoint; he or she becomes more of a *person*—outside the workplace as well as in it. In the past, we have accepted the possibility of artists, actors, and professionals finding fulfillment and excitement in their work, but we expected most workers to be content with limited, dehumanizing jobs. Today, however, "working for the corporation" can open the door to meaningful, integrated lives.

Down-to-Earth Beginning

We tend to search for institutional ways of leaping to utopia, but no one is going to rescue the American worker from all the troubles of life. No schemes will correct all of society's wrongs. A strong community has to be built on strong individuals, and that is a slow development process. "Human development won't be achieved by forming some form of commune where we all love eath other. It requires growth in our society as it is," says Stan Lundine, former mayor of Jamestown, New York, a city in which labor, management, and civic leaders pulled a divided community with a declining economy back together.[1]

Some people are well-developed, having been shaped by family, friends, teachers, and others, before they come to the workplace for the first time. Unfortunately, many have either not developed as healthy individuals or they have done so only to find they have to surrender themselves to fit the job situation. A caring company does many things to nurture its human resources—whatever their stage of development when they are employed. It is more likely than other companies are to have career counseling, in-house training open to anyone who feels challenged to participate in it, college tuition refunds—even for non–work-related courses, performance appraisal procedures, and other features that encourage people to grow and to test themselves.

There are numerous offices and plants in the United States where a visitor can immediately sense that employees are glad to be there. The spirit of a productive organization is nearly visible or tangible. Employees exude enthusiasm about what they are doing, what they are learning, the improvements they are making, the better job the company is doing. They are eager to show visitors their work stations and describe what it is they are doing and what they hope to do next. Many people, however, do not share this excitement. They were not helped to develop the capacity for it by their family or other institutions along the way. For them, the workplace may be the first exposure to the possibility of having self-respect. If they are fortunate enough to be in the right place, they may find both an atmosphere in which their having self-respect is important to someone else and the climate for nurturing it. In small steps, people learn to set goals, learn the necessary skills to improve their performance, and get feedback that tells them they are moving ahead. Little by little they become individuals rather than invalids. Little by little the organization that might have rented only their body shows that it is interested in the investment of their spirit.

Winning Self-Esteem

Participative or humanistic management begins with nurturing people's self-esteem and aims toward self-actualization. Self-esteem enables a person to work better with others because he does not have to be on the defensive and contrive ways to look like a winner. Self-actualization comes with the ability to balance the need for belonging with the need to stand out as an individual. In the workplace, an individual's me-ism or narcissism can be turned toward a more healthy pursuit of self-development as he or she learns to accept responsibility by seeing how it affects relationships. Too much of life can be structured in ways that prevent people from seeing the impact of their actions on others, and they don't see the efforts that are required to provide the things they might take for granted. The well-structured workplace provides quick, direct feedback on actions and reactions. Other institutions may preach what people ought to, but the workplace offers the test of the market through which people can learn the value of what they do.

Not only do business corporations (and other workplaces) have the motivation to deal with human resources development, but many of them have the means for doing a good job of it. Today, they can train people in ways that make them individuals. It is to the corporation's advantage as well as the individual's to avoid training that works toward making people similar and interchangeable. The old-style training that so many millions of workers have endured is essentially the following: "Here's what you do. Now watch me. Here's how you do it. Now you do it." In humanistic or participative settings, development is far more individually tailored, even at the lowest-level jobs. The worker is given a broad view of what his or her job is, where it fits into the scheme of things at least in terms of the immediately surrounding or related jobs. The tone of the training is "here's what we are trying to accomplish and why."

Personal growth is a process of winning—not necessarily spectacular victories but small, day-by-day wins, sometimes accompanied by losses. In some workplaces today, people are raising themselves to levels of performance and discovering talents that they might never have realized elsewhere. They are becoming winners. The sense of doing and winning propels them along the road of self-development. Although schemes for providing workers a pat on the back have been tried in the past, workers know when recognition comes from genuine regard for genuine accomplishments and when it is merely manipulation to get them to perform work they really don't want to do. Productivity must have some personal dimension for the worker. For example, the person turning out 100 widgets per day may be productive according to economic measures. If he produces 110 widgets, he is even more productive. But neither level gives him the feeling of personal worth unless he knows his own skill has been responsible for the good performance.

Productivity—personal or corporate—is of no concern to some people. They do not have enough self-esteem to care whether they are productive, and their poor work behavior is perceived as a "lack of work ethic." It's common to assume that a person should have the work ethic by the time he or she reaches working age or there is no hope for his becoming productive—that the company can't do what the family and schools have failed to do. To say that once a person reaches the workplace he will learn no new attitudes defies what many of us have seen to the contrary, however. Just as people can be pulled aside and taught the wrong things by disgruntled fellow-workers, a new employee can learn positive values and attitudes in the workplace.

The workplace dominates many people's lives in terms of the hours spent there and in terms of the leadership—formal and informal—that affects them directly. It has always been the case that the old hands show the newcomer what sort of behavior is acceptable in a particular workplace. If their own self-esteem is low and they are not committed to organizational goals, they will show the newcomer how to knock off early, look busy at the right times, and cut corners to meet quotas. Even workers who are interested in doing the job well may show the newcomer how to beat the system in order to succeed. They will share tricks such as double-ordering of parts and supplies so they'll have enough of what they need or how to abuse equipment to get greater output. Although much of the worker's value-shaping is done by peers and immediate supervisors, the moral tone and the values of the organization is set to a large degree by top management. Managers and workers down the line watch the upper echelons to see what pays off and what doesn't. We have come to expect workers to learn some shady practices on the job. Why, then, should we be surprised that they can learn positive values there as well? And it *is* happening.

Because the workplace is results-oriented, it is no place for losers. It quickly signals when behavior is unproductive, antisocial, or self-defeating. The more the quality of work depends on the worker's discretion, the more it depends on discipline that comes from within. In earlier times, people could be made to do a minimum of work through the discipline imposed by the boss. Today's effective organization has to be adaptive—a learning organism—but the people in it cannot learn unless they have self-discipline. The person who hasn't disciplined himself to concentrate on learning to read, for example, can't read the destination signs on the bus that would take him to work. He is a prisoner of his ignorance. He is not self-reliant. He is not free.

Freedom at work comes from being able to be responsible for one's own actions in meeting reality's tests. The person who can't control himself in a given environment can exert no control over that environment. The alienation he then feels results in negative behavior—a desperate attempt to assert freedom and power that he does not really have. People are learning that freedom is won through development and performance; it is not granted by someone else. Freedom begins with acceptance of limitations and rising above them. In some workplaces, peers and supervisors are helping people lift themselves to greater self-esteem and freedom by helping them learn to learn. An important part of the humanistic–participative trend in business today is the conveyance of skills that enable people to be productive and thereby want to relate positively to the organization.

Traditionally, many workers have acquired only the minimum skills they need for doing some narrowly defined job. They cannot readily move to another job, and they have little control over the one they are doing. But some companies, today, are broadening the base of workers' skills and giving them enough of an overview of the situation in which they are working so they can control the process rather than being controlled by it. In auto plants, for example, some operations now have a control button which any worker on the line may hit to halt the process if he or she sees something going wrong. At Kimberly–Clark Corporation, more than 1,000 employees at seven different mills have been through a new training program that aims at several objectives that develop more skilled and more motivated workers. Employees are trained not only to know what they are to do in terms of tasks but also why they are doing it. Workers in manufacturing and warehousing operations are trained not only to operate but to control the process. They are trained to know the tasks and problems of other crew members.

At the Skippy Peanut Butter plant in Little Rock, Arkansas, each worker has the opportunity to learn all the jobs in the plant. Employees do not have job descriptions; there are no inspectors or supervisors. They are given extensive information about all aspects of the plant's operation. When a new worker is hired, he is shown a career path laid out for several years. From then on, he is continually challenged to learn about one job after another. Monthly skills testing and proficiency certification determine his salary raises. Work assignments are determined by teams of workers since there are no supervisors.

Stressing the Individual

The skeptic may say the so-called freedom found in the corporate world is a token freedom bestowed on those who conform to the organization's rules. The self-development force which is driving so many workers today wouldn't tolerate this sort of tokenism, however. People reject false offerings and rebel at the lack of genuine regard for them, thereby denying the corporation the free, creative workforce that it must have to attain its objectives. Fewer and fewer people will accept the "organizational imperative" which placed the organization above the individual.[2] They are now more likely to regard the organization as something that exists for the benefit of the individual.

Until recently, Americans have generally seen the corporation as a threat to their personal freedom. The search for freedom has too often meant the freedom *from* work rather than freedom through work. Some people, especially during the recent me-ism years, have been so concerned with protecting their freedom they were not involved in the world; they isolated themselves from it. The workplace, however, is beginning to lead them back to involvement—to attending to their community and esteem needs so they can proceed toward genuine self-fulfillment.

Skeptics of what is happening in participative corporations have concentrated their attack on the notion of community or "team-building." To them, the rising spirit of cooperation looks like a resurrection of the old organizational imperative. They do not see that some corporations are responding to the rising "individual imperative" which calls for people's being permitted to realize their individual potential. The companies that are winning today and building for the future depend on individual skills as well as on teamwork. They know that teamwork means little if the team is made up of weak individuals. A football guard, for example, makes his contribution not with team spirit alone; he develops blocking and tackling skills, speed, and strength that are his, not the team's. Alvin Toffler points out that the industrial system required a standardized workforce and led Karl Marx to assume that all workers would come to see themselves as part of "the working masses." But Marx is being stood on his head, says Toffler, because we don't need thousands of workers doing standardized jobs. "What the system needs are workers who are resourceful, innovative, educated, even individualistic."[3]

Employee participation and involvement efforts build both the individual and the group. They do not employ a "herd" psychology. Although many futurists have presented visions of a future in which the group ego takes precedence over the individual, we are now looking at a new kind of individual and a new kind of group. Early industrialization made people interchangeable cogs in a vast machine. But this stage of American industrialization is reversing that trend. As work becomes more abstract and creative, people become less and less a faceless workforce. They develop their individual talents, make their own special contributions, and receive recognition as separate persons.

The trends in job redesign and organizational relationships can turn us back from collectivism. As people satisfy higher and higher levels of needs, their cases become more individualized. Because workers are not all alike, James O'Toole of the University of Southern California, an expert in the world of work, sugggests several new rules for treating people humanistically: offer a broad selection of tasks requiring varying levels of commitment, abilities, supervision, and time for completion; permit them to select the jobs that meet their particular needs; accommodate differences in their off-the-job commitments; and allow people to move laterally and even downward if they so choose.[4]

Development of the individual is a broadening process. People generally try to narrow their life focus to fit into a rigidly structured system, however. Youth worry about the one right educational path or the one right occupation to aim for. They struggle to determine the one thing they are good at or the thing that they do best. Some, but not all, later realize their greater potential lies in combining a number of talents and interests. Too many spend their lives trying to cast themselves into a tight mold. This tendency is being overcome as corporations seek to eliminate the maze of job classifications that limit what a person can do and restrict, not only corporate effectiveness, but the opportunity for individuals to grow.

New technology can assist in people's development. Secretaries have learned to operate word processors and go on to become computer department supervisors. One woman, who handled an average of sixty phone calls a day to schedule the use of a large corporation's conference rooms, suggested that a computer could do the job better. Management bought her idea. She had suggested herself out of that job but propelled herself into some training which led to more interesting, less computer-like work in the company.

People don't have to move on to new jobs to grow. A few firms, like Weyerhaeuser Company, for example, are experimenting with raising workers' pay as they acquire new skills even if those skills aren't required in their present jobs. A person may select a team membership after studying the available jobs—sometimes by viewing a videotape. He or she will then float from one assignment to another within a work team; pay for mastering each functional area of a team's activities is approved by vote of the other team members. Pay for knowledge reflects a long-term view of the payoffs from investment in human resources.

Tender Individualism

Just as we are born and die as individuals, we are hired, fired, and retired as individuals—but along the way, in the workplace or wherever we act out our lives, we find we are interdependent with others. When people clamor for independence, what they may really be asking for is recognition and the opportunity to express their feelings of interdependence. They may be crying to escape isolation rather than to attain it. Denying one's interdependence with others does not make for freedom. The fellow who speeds out into traffic and charges through a red light may feel he is free and independent, but he is highly dependent on others' watching out for him. A person can attain more real independence by recognizing his dependence, says Fred Herzberg. We reduce our opportunity for freedom by trying to maintain an illusion of complete independence, he says.

The more jobs are expanded in the number of tasks involved and the more they are self-managed by the worker, the more people recognize their interdependence with others. When they are truly interested in good performance as individuals, they find they can produce better results by helping one another than by working at cross-purposes. They must rely on someone to produce the materials and equipment they use. Salespeople must rely on others to produce the goods they sell. And all are dependent on the customer. Not all work is performed by groups or teams, but numerous relationships—up, down, and sideways—determine the effectiveness of the individual and of the organization. A growing person discovers the need to cooperate with others who have different talents or who possess certain information. Self-reliance leads to mutual reliance. Even the lone scientist must rely on others to produce his research equipment, his laboratory, and even to provide his education. Great scientific breakthroughs are generally the result of the brilliant efforts of an individual who stands on the shoulders of brilliant individuals of the past and who shares ideas and information with brilliant contemporaries. As increased cooperation improves workers' chances of winning, it lessens their need to assert false independence.

"Rugged individualism" meets neither the need for social harmony and cooperation nor the requirements for self-development. Waving the banner for individualism and independence does not appeal to people who are concerned about *individuation*—developing their unique, individual traits rather than being concerned about being a separate entity. The emerging paradigm or new image of man places a high priority on forming distinct individuals within a greater unity. This is individuation, not individualism. It does not elevate the individual over the group but it does elevate the individual within the group. It calls for a *tender individualism* that permits a person to distinguish himself or herself as an individual while maintaining the highest respect for others. It eases the pain of that troublesome duality that pits man, the individual, against man, the social animal.

Freedom within the whole is more fitting to people's new image of themselves. We can have no freedom unless we are competent to address the forces around us, and this includes other people. "What freedom was to the eighteenth century, wholism will be to the twentieth," says Barbara Marx Hubbard.[5] Two decades earlier, William H. Whyte noted that individualism is impossible—that Americans never really practiced it as the myths would have us believe.[6] The concept of individualism is an inadequate moral base even for a morality centered on the individual, much less for one centered on society or a deity. Human growth is proving to be of greater moral power because it leads to self-reliance as well as to reliance on and concern for others.

The Need for Community

Within any organization there will be informal groups and relationships. The informal community—even if it offers only the chance to gripe together—is one of the few things that some people have valued in their jobs. This sense of community sometimes rivals that of the family. For many people, no other institution offers the potential for a sense of belonging. For people not concerned about self-development, this belongingness may be the principal benefit of working. But a fair day's pay and a little fellowship do not meet all the needs of the growing number of people who are interested in exploring their full potential.

The gripe group is not likely to lead to individuation or personal growth. In fact, it represents a retreat from the self, a surrender to the group, and abandonment of the hope to grow. A person is more likely to be developing when he feels his group and his larger organization are in harmony, working toward some agreed-upon objective and doing a good job of proceeding toward it. A group such as a quality circle may display signs in its work area headed with some name: "Busy Bees," "Inner Circle," "Dirty Dozen," "Flashie Finishers," "Swinging Signals," etc. But along with slogans and photos of members are statistical charts tracing progress toward some goal the group has selected to work toward. Good feelings and a little fun are the by-product of being committed to the job. Some of these work groups have become so supportive of the individual members that people have sometimes declined opportunities to work in other departments or other companies because the bond of respect has grown so strong.

In a participative setting, the small group can give the individual more personalized feedback on performance while large, formal organizations can do little beyond giving occasional recognition. Better reinforcement of good behavior comes through ongoing relationships with fellow workers. At the same time, however, the participative situation helps link the small group to the total organization. It's not easy for a worker to feel totally involved with a 300-acre plant and 10,000 fellow workers. It seems natural for people to confine their trust and fellowship to close associates and keep other members of the larger organization at arm's length, but participation in the problem-solving process may encourage them to develop more contacts in order to acquire information and establish working relationships with others in the company. Being better informed about the broader scope of operations leads workers to expand their commitments to more and more persons in the total organization.

In participative companies, both the setting of objectives and the attainment of them depend on a chain of overlapping circles of interest, planning, reporting, suggesting, and problem solving. Rather than a chain of command, today's successful corporation fashions a chain of mutuality. One member of a work team in a Tennessee textile plant says the participative process at her company "is the best way I know to make an 'It's not my responsibility' attitude obsolete."

Many people have a deep need to relate to others, but if togetherness becomes the primary objective of the group, rigidities can set in and work against the health of the individual. When there are specific work objectives for the group to work toward, however, the group becomes a support for individual growth. As the individual commits more of himself to group objectives, he feels the sense of community more deeply. Cooperation comes through enlightened self-interest. When people aren't growing, however, they desperately try to seek relative gains by tearing others down, discrediting their efforts, and resisting progress in the organization.

Whyte feared the social ethic and pointed out that the organization or system was so beneficent and alluring that people made an imperative of belonging. He warned about allowing any single organization to capture our sense of belonging.[7] Blind loyalty to the company has declined since the 1950s, however. People are more likely to attach their loyalties to particular persons or groups or to their own profession. If they are loyal to the company, it is likely to be because they feel they are genuine members, not subjects pledging their allegiance from afar. Today, in fact, a person's contribution to the work situation may be enhanced by the skills, contacts, and knowledge acquired through association with other organizations outside the job. In turn, development as an effective individual at work increases his or her value to people outside the workplace.

Person-to-Person Skills

Corporate training has traditionally dealt with the technical skills needed for performing some particular task, but one of the major areas of skills deficiency today has to do with interpersonal relations—the ability to show care, concern, and courtesy. What looks like poor work attitudes often stems from the lack of social skills. For example, the store clerk who shakes her head and walks away in response to a customer's question is not necessarily hostile. She may be afraid of dealing with strangers and lack the simple social skills of looking someone in the eye and speaking clearly. These shortcomings dampen that person's self-esteem and make the work an unpleasant experience. Needless to say, that's not good for the company's business.

More and more training is now being addressed to these needs, helping workers blossom into more secure and effective persons. Banks and retail stores are videotaping tellers and clerks in both simulated and real-life situations and then letting individuals learn by watching themselves. In manufacturing plants, where most employees do not come into contact with customers, anyone from blue-collar and white-collar hourly workers to engineers and senior managers can be taught to understand how a person's behavior is perceived by others and how to be aware of what others are really saying behind their words and actions. They are being taught how to define problems and work cooperatively toward solutions. In the past, training in interpersonal skills was confined primarily to managers and sales personnel, but now the rewards of exposing all employees to it are becoming apparent.

Training can help people view their work in a far more meaningful way. Dr. Clayton Lafferty, psychologist and chief executive officer of Human Synergistics, uses the example of two auto service department managers to illustrate how people might view the same job in negative terms or positive ones. One manager sees the stream of incoming cars as being driven by people with problems; his role, he feels, is to diagnose those problems; he sees himself as a sort of physician. The other manager sees each car coming in as being driven by a person with a gripe; he approaches each customer with dread. For one of these managers, work is a challenge—an opportunity to help. For the other, the same work is an endless source of irritaion.

New training programs are also helping supervisors and managers become better leaders. One foreman was about to lose his job—be fired or, at least, demoted—because of his poor leadership ability, but participating in a new quality circle and undergoing the related training improved his leadership skills. His boss now regards him as one of the most effective foremen in the company.

Skills to Carry Home

The life skills being learned by individuals in the corporation have started a ripple effect from the workplace to the family, local organizations, and the greater society. Many of the skills learned in work situations are applicable to the individual's nonwork life. Dr. Lafferty, for example, has helped airline agents learn to deal with disgruntled passengers. When the worker can learn to handle a problem situation from the customer's perspective and acquire the skills for taking the steam out of someone whose luggage has been lost, he or she can use those skills for getting along with family and neighbors, he says.

In *The Third Wave*, Toffler says the family could be strengthened again by people working at home.[8] While this may be possible for some, there is far more potential for people coming alive at work and transferring their values and skills to home life. People are already bringing home views and skills for dealing more effectively with their spouses and children. When respect and commitment are nurtured at work, jobholders acquire the vital ingredients for a sound marriage and family. Richard Walton, at the Harvard Business School, has seen, too, that the skills learned on the job can help persons in their family life. Women employees, for example, who have gained decision-making experience have changed from passive to more active roles at home. Many workers have improved their listening skills—an asset in family relations.[9]

When Emmett began coming home and revealing the excitement generated in a quality circle at work, his wife suggested that he apply what he was learning there to improving the quality of life at home. Each of them had brought three children to their marriage, and something needed to be done to forge a new family. The answer was a family quality circle with the parents and children meeting every Sunday afternoon to hash out their problems. Emmett was able to convey enough of the techniques in defining problems, brainstorming solutions, and working toward agreement that even his four-year-old son was able to contribute to better understanding and relations.

Ray was a C student in high school, belonged to no clubs, held no class offices. Over the past twenty years, he has worked in several factories and become a fairly good machine operator. He has never expected more from the job than a reasonable paycheck. During the past two years, he has been a member of an action team. He has met many times with his fellow workers to analyze problems that have impaired the quality of the auto parts they produce. He has even met several times with upper management to present the group's suggested solutions. Last year, his team's presentation to management was so impressive the company paid the team's way to a major conference on quality of worklife to make its presentation publicly. Ray and his team have also visited several vendor plants to talk about the quality level and delivery times on the components with which his team works. They have even visited a competitor's plant to glean ideas for improving their own department. The opportunity to travel, make public speeches, and develop solutions to business or technical problems has given Ray a sense of fulfillment he never dreamed of.

Over twenty years as a management magazine editor, I have had my share of plant tours and briefings. Generally, the briefings are done either by top management or sharp young managers or staff persons. In recent years, however, I have heard a number of presentations by teams of workers—mixes of mountain men, blacks with Afro haircuts, women whom you might picture at home rocking a grandchild, and high school dropouts making desperate attempts to grow beards. Their grammar was sometimes far better than I expected, sometimes not. Their stage presence was sometimes far better than I expected, sometimes not. But their enthusiasm and resourcefulness consistently surpassed my most generous expectations. These were people who had come alive at work.

The workplace can also contribute to a person's wholeness by leading him or her well beyond the workplace into participation in civic activities. Some companies encourage involvement in outside activities and even provide corporate equipment or facilities for community work. At Honeywell Inc., for instance, a few quality circles have moved on from productivity and quality problems to activities in the community such as sponsorship of "Olympics" for "special children." It seems a natural progression that people who are developing will move from quality-of-product and quality-of-worklife considerations to the broader quality-of-life interests.

Some companies have begun granting time off with pay to employees who are nearing retirement so they can participate in civic activities. Xerox Corporation grants special leaves of absence for employees to engage in social service work. They help build shelters for the needy, teach office skills to the blind, and help handicapped persons find jobs. Individuals propose their own projects, and a committee of employees evaluates the proposals and determines whether leave is to be granted.

These kinds of personal involvement in community affairs put social action back into the hands of the individual. Through such one-on-one relationships, the corporation can contribute more to meeting its social responsibilities than through direct contributions of dollars. The expertise of corporate management and professional workers plus the talents and time of workers at all levels could mount a substantial attack on the nation's social problems.

The Individual in Control

Today's world problems overwhelm people who don't see how they can make any individual contribution to solving them. They need to feel they are in control of part of their lives, at least. They want to be able to chip away at their corner of the world. Too often, they lack a sense of the future and confidence that they could do anything to influence it. Learning to set objectives and work toward them in the workplace is a healthy start at orienting people to the future and to concerns outside themselves. Within the scope of their skills and information, they can prioritize problems and study ways to deal with them.

The questions of how to govern a society in which no one individual or party is in control—of how to reach consensus in an era of diversity—may be answered in the workplace. Our governmental processes are changing slowly, if at all, but the corporation is becoming more adaptive and exploring new ways to tap people's talents. The movement toward broader participation at work may provide lessons for the dispersal of decision-making power in society.

The corporation may enable people to find their way to decentralization and true democratization. When I have asked members of quality circles or action teams how they reach agreement without taking a vote, as is always the case, I have been surprised to learn that they have found ways to work through differences of opinion until all members see the preferred course of action. The same is true at the upper levels of some corporations where executives work out broad corporate strategies and objectives. People are learning in the workplace to examine their own ideas and weigh them against those of others. As they develop abilities to deal with complex social relationships, they will be well on their way toward new styles of participation in the politics of the larger arena. The ability to set and achieve personal and corporate goals orients people toward the future—a vital ingredient in sound governance. As they learn the discipline and skills to be self-reliant, they will not have to fear a future of determinism. They can do more at the individual or community levels to determine the problems and issues they want to address, make policy decisions, and administer solutions.

Richard Walton says that, in the cases he has observed, "when individuals are able to use a broader range of skills and abilities in their work, they tend to see themselves as capable of making a larger variety of contributions to their community." On the other hand, he has noted, "human constriction at work is conducive to human constriction in other societal settings."[10]

Permitting people to truly distinguish themselves from one another may enable us to avert heading toward a monolithic society. Individuation produces diversity, not sameness. Raw individualism, on the other hand, holds people apart and renders them vulnerable to domination by other powers. The self-interest described by Adam Smith is not sufficient for social life or even for the economic system, says Michael Novak. "Narrowly construed, self-interest alone counsels caution and self-protection. In order to be creative—to venture into new areas, to experiment, to pioneer—one must be willing to lose what one has, to replace security with insecurity."[11]

Developments within the corporation today could also help us turn back from being an overly competitive, adversarial, litigious society which stands a poor chance of making progress in human or economic terms. The old adversarial relationship between labor and management, for example, often prevents the flow and implementation of new ideas that are needed to make the organization competitive. Both sides are beginning to acknowledge that they have to serve their common interest through more day-to-day cooperation.

As the corporation helps people develop themselves and nurtures positive human values, the healthier human climate may draw the traditional, value-shaping institutions back into more active roles. The family and schools will support those values that pay off in the workplace. A more human work climate would mean the churches would not have to try to bridge the gap between people's work and their "higher" calling. They would neither have to ignore the work world nor preach escape from it. They could, instead, show the way to meaningful, personal growth and simultaneous involvement in the social and economic problems of humankind. If people gain identity and a sense of community through their work and relationships at work, they will be able to turn to religion out of fullness rather than emptiness. They can turn to their god in good times, not seek him only as a refuge in bad times.

Changes in individual needs and changes in corporate needs are reshaping the workplace in sharp contrast not only to early industrial times but to the situation in the 1960s and 1970s. These changes are making it possible for workers to move:

from acceptance of repetitive and closely defined work, through a disinterest in the available work, toward commitment to work suitable for human growth

from self-denial, through self-indulgence, toward self-development

from submissiveness, through rebelliousness, toward participation in organizations that one can expect to influence

from slavery to the clock, through absenteeism and tardiness, toward improved attendance at interesting work and flexible schedules that permit more integrated lives

from reliance on a boss, through dependence on the system, toward self reliance and reliance on fellow workers

from low skills, through highly specialized technical skills, toward technical plus interpersonal skills

People have an increasing chance of joining the ranks of the new achievers as they undergo movement from the past, through the turbulent present, toward a better future.

PART III
MANAGING
HUMAN GROWTH

11

The Quality of Management

THE WORKER'S SUCCESS IN PURSUING THE DEVELOPMENT ETHIC and the corporation's ability to improve quality and productivity are linked in a common fate. To a great degree, that fate is determined by the character of the people in management positions. Management of the future, if it is to have any role at all, will have to link the human and the economic factors into a meaningful whole.

There is plenty of justification for being skeptical about managers' being an instrument for human growth. Managers, in turn, are often skeptical about people's potential for being more committed to effective work. The stalemate can be broken only if management makes some giant leap upward in its perception and purpose. There are signs, in fact, that economic realities are forcing them to examine their traditional approach to business. However, the fact that management is in the lead in sensing the new paradigm and appreciating the new values should give us even more hope for economic and human growth.

Over the past quarter-century, the trend in scientific, financially oriented management has run in the opposite direction to the values people have been expressing. While management was perfecting its quantitative approach to business, people were coming around to qualitative concerns.

A dozen or so years ago, I was as intrigued as anyone with the prospect of management's becoming a profession based on a technology for managing organizations. Management had once been essentially a seat-of-the-pants activity and had, perhaps, been elevated to an art by a few especially gifted managers. But that seems too crude for these sophisticated, complex times. I looked on the "near-profession" of management with its technological and financial skills as the hope of the future. Now, however, managers themselves are beginning to suspect that their own orientation has been wrong. Overreliance on their bag of management skills has generated a management corps whose culture is too limited to deal with fast-changing global realities. Where seat-of-the-pants had been too crude in its techniques, "scientific management" now seems too limited in its scope.

With the dawning of the 1980s, U.S. management began undergoing serious self-examination in terms of its practices, style, and objectives. In January, 1980, at a meeting sponsored by the consulting firm Booz Allen & Hamilton, nearly 100 top executives heard from other executives, government officials, and professors about industry's sorest ailment and current buzzword—productivity. The theme, different from the flood of other conferences on that topic, was perhaps best expressed by Harvard professor Robert Hayes. United States management had become too oriented to the financial side of the business, especially in the short term, he said.[1] Six months later, Dr. Hayes and William Abernathy published an article entitled "Managing Our Way to Economic Decline" in the *Harvard Business Review* which managers were discussing for years to come.[2] One of their principal assertions: Poor economic performance in the United States was due to management's failure to maintain technological competence in product and production processes.

Headcounts and Overhead

During the 1960s and 1970s, U.S. mangement had concentrated on marketing and finance rather than on the product and the production processes. It had developed ways of screening out the human element in order to make its world more controllable. It managed the numbers and manipulated (or ignored) people. Numbers can be used to describe the world in limited ways, but too many managers came to regard numbers as reality itself. As a result, they tended to see workers not as multidimensional beings, but as headcounts and overhead.

The education, work experience, and incentives for managers

created a corporate leadership that was far removed from the heart of the business. People at the top rarely understood the markets, products, and production processes well enough to have the necessary insights for big leaps forward in quality and productivity. In place of entrepreneurs with vision, dedication, and intimate knowledge of the business, had come legions of professional managers who were analytical, cautious, and manipulative.

For decades, the top management of U.S. corporations has concentrated on one narrow focus or another which served as poor substitutes for a total, strategic view of its mission. In the 1950s, top management had been predominantly operations- or production-oriented; its focus was too inward. By the 1960s, many companies found they could accelerate their growth by taking on a marketing orientation. The managers who had the most influence were those who could tune in to people's wants, intensify them, and shape products accordingly. Ironically, however, the pace of true innovation slowed during those years. After all, potential customers ask only for new products that they can envision; the marketer's response rarely generates the great leaps forward that an inventor or entrepreneur can bring to the marketplace. Still another shift in focus occurred through the 1960s as executives with financial and legal backgrounds moved to the top to preserve what had been created earlier or rearrange corporate entities.

Management expertise became more and more a collection of analysis and control techniques and less and less a matter of creativity. "... [O]ur reaction—indeed overreaction—to complexity has been to impose a system, and the result has been an artificially satisfying sensation that order has somehow been restored to our universe," says Mary Cunningham, herself the master of management systems and planning as she rocketed to fame in Bendix Corporation. "As a result we have become the victims of the systems we have created. Computers, forecasting models, organization charts, and new methods of quantification have been idealized as solutions. Business has become austere and stifling."[3]

Many managers thus acquired the ability to find problems—to spot the financially weak operating unit in a company or the product that is not returning enough on the investment dedicated to it. With its lack of detailed knowledge of the business, upper management is unable to do more than detect the fact that there are problems. It does not have the operating experience and know-how to understand the possible causes or suggest remedies. The numbers signal when something may not be right, but someone has to provide solutions in the real world of products, machines, and people. The numbers can help management judge an operation's past performance, but they don't reflect what its potential is for future development.

Too often, an executive with a corporate dollar to invest has been inclined to buy another company rather than gamble on the development of truly new products or capabilities of the present company. The manager who needs a boost in revenues in order to look good is apt to go on the acquisition trail. That's why many companies have poured more money into the conglomerization of old companies than they have invested in research and development or employee training. Far too many managers have come to see their companies as "money machines" rather than as engines for the generation of quality products. They have substituted financial analysis and the manipulation of corporate chess pieces for technological leadership and innovation in the heart of the business.

To their dismay, however, analyses show that conglomerates have generally not performed as well for the stockholders as have companies that concentrated on one market or one area of technology and carefully fitted their operations together. Innovation, quality, and productivity have suffered. "Nothing is more interesting for a financially trained executive than working on acquisitions, but they benefit only the few who have organized them," admits one chief executive who once engaged in that game himself. It is not surprising that when management devotes its attention to managing portfolios of corporate entities it cannot dedicate itself to leading the organization to new generations of products and production processes.

The process of merging or avoiding mergers has drained both financial resources and morale from the companies involved. In 1982, four major companies waged a costly acquisition war. Bendix Corporation fired the first shot with a low bid offer for Martin Marietta Corporation, which borrowed nearly a billion dollars to counter in an attempt to buy Bendix. United Technologies Corp. joined in bidding for Bendix, agreeing that, if it acquired Bendix, it would divide the spoils with Martin Marietta. At one point in the struggle, Bendix owned 70 percent of Martin Marietta, which owned 46 percent of Bendix.

Bill Agee, chairman of Bendix, got Allied Corporation to come to his rescue. That ended the fighting, but the Agee victory soon paled. Discovering he then had no real job and a dubious future, he left the presidency of Allied within months. Agee had been the bright star of management when he became chairman of Bendix at age thirty-eight in 1972. Now, his merger tactics and subsequent departure via a $4 million "golden parachute" became the symbol of merger mania and its disuptive effect on the corporation. Nearly forty U.S. and foreign banks tied up more than $5.5 billion to back the four companies' war. The companies themselves represented more than $8 billion in stockholders' equity.

Many people questioned whether the final outcome had created better corporate entities. The issue was already heated by giant mergers of the previous year when DuPont made the $6.8 billion acquisition of Conoco Inc., United States Steel Corporation bought Marathon Oil Company for $6.2 billion, and Standard Oil Co. (Ohio) acquired Kennecott Corp. for $1.8 billion. Had any of these companies become stronger in their main lines of business? How much management time had been expended in fighting for control of the companies they had acquired or sometimes not succeeded in acquiring? What was the negative impact of all the activity on the workforces of those companies? What was the cost in terms of insecurity suffered for many months to come by managers wondering if and when they could be axed as corporate structures were rearranged?

Management's preoccupation with acquiring and arranging companies has often led to collections of facilities and people with no common core of technology, no common objectives, and no common values. Rather than creating a critical mass which could have spawned innovation, they often unwittingly destroyed the creativity that had existed in the original units. It is difficult to blend corporate cultures and values systems; as a result, many companies that try to diversify through acquisitions wind up as little more than conglomerates, observes Kenichi Ohmae.[4] A sound, diversified company exploits synergies, but conglomerates set their objectives in strictly financial terms and lack a unifying force other than a common financial statement.

"Manageering" a Career

Quantitative-minded managers have not concerned themselves with such things as "unifying force." Instead of managing the people and the "product," more and more people *manageered* careers for themselves. They sought the tools needed to win at the numbers game and skirted past the fundamental job of delivering products and services. Major universities intensified the pace by developing a body of skills for playing that game. In the years when management was becoming alarmed about people's self-centeredness and lack of a work ethic, many managers were busily pursuing their own brand of narcissism.

"A manager is a manager is a manager." That popular misconception drew many people to the false profession of management where mastering the numbers propelled one up the ladder of success. Increasingly, in the postwar years, managers were able to move from division to division, company to company, and industry to industry. They became highly mobile with their transferable financial and administrative skills. For years, managers got by—in fact, did well—by producing the right numbers, but their focus on the short term finally caught up with them. Their failure to produce quality in the real world showed up in the customer dissatisfaction and poor productivity which resulted partly from lack of long-term investments of money and talent and partly from lack of commitment by managers as well as nonmanagers. While certain portable skills are essential, a manager must also know his or her company's product, production processes, production people, and sales people if that manager is going to attain quality goals in the real world of product and service.

Focusing on the short term led to efforts to preserve the status quo rather than build organizations that could meet change. In time, an accumulation of short-term outlooks and actions caught up with many companies. Many managers had their eye on the bottom line, but a funny thing happened on the way to the bottom line. So many ingredients of good business had been eliminated in the middle that both the bottom line—profits—and the top line—revenue—failed to grow as expected and often declined alarmingly.

Too many managers tended to look at a given operation with an eye toward squeezing costs out of it. Wherever possible, they tried to design out the human factors of production and distribution, overlooking the fact that the route to competitiveness lies in innovation and that innovation depends on people. In boom times, when almost any mistakes would be hidden by skyrocketing growth, an individual could detach himself from his mistakes by playing the stepping-stone game and moving on to another job before his mistakes were realized or his cost-cutting efforts drained the company of long-term strength. But those days ended in the late 1970s. A relatively few exceptional managers, on the other hand, sought ways to expand the possibilities for their operations. They educated their workforce, structured meaningful work for them, and provided a community to which they could become full members; their organizations became more vital and innovative.

As companies tightened their belts during those recession years, approaches to cost reduction distinguished the more humanistic or participative companies from the hierarchical companies. The former were building for the future while the hierarchical ones generally robbed the future. Humanistic companies were coming up with substantial savings suggested and worked out by committed, well-informed employees at all levels. Their workforces delivered ideas for both measurable and immeasurable savings in the cost of doing business and winning new business. In the traditional approach to cost reduction, management generally assigned special cost cutters to work away at the numbers, oblivious to the way their actions lowered the effectiveness of people trying to accomplish the company's fundamental work. The things people do to compensate for substandard purchased materials, poorly maintained equipment, inadequate supplies, and cost-control paperwork may actually raise costs. And the entire effort is likely to damage the quality of product or service. People pressured to get the job done within severe limitations fight with their counterparts in other departments; client relationships break down. The more management tries to get things under control and fight a holding action against eroding business, the more employees—including many of the managers—fight a withholding action. To say the least, they do not give their best.

As the 1980s opened, then, we heard chief executives, especially of the larger and better firms, question management practices, style, and objectives. They had begun to realize that their short-term orientation had been harmful in many ways. They recognized their own lack of technological insights and closeness to the customer—two fundamentals of doing business. They were losing the battle to foreign competitors and failing to lay the foundations for the industries of tomorrow.

It has become painfully apparent that our technology and the institutions for delivering it have lost headway. Corporate management needs to make smart investments in research and development that will lead to improved products, new products, new means of production, and even new industries. The corporation needs more top-management involvement in operating decisions, more technology planning folded into corporate strategy, and more people development as part of its thrust. If the people in leadership positions are uncomfortable with the technology on which their companies depend and with other factors at the core of the business, the corporation is limited in its potential for growth or even for survival. Without technical insight, leaders cannot visualize what the next generation of products will be. The person who doesn't understand the industry's competitive situation is unlikely to recognize where tomorrow's competition will come from in this time of technological upheaval.

This Time Around

In recent years, some companies have taken measures to work technology assessment into the information base for fashioning their corporate strategy. There are signs, too, that a scientific or technical background is providing more managers an edge in moving toward the top of the company. With the competitive challenge from abroad, as well as from here at home, American corporations will soon come back around to management emphasis on production, engineering, and other functions that relate directly to the heart of the business.

In manufacturing companies, especially, the "key problem for the 1980s and beyond will remain how to manage under conditions of increasing technical ferment," say Abernathy, Clark, and Kantrow.[5] In *Industrial Renaissance*, they argue convincingly that U.S. companies have lost the ability to improve their manufacturing process while other manufacturers have come forth with new technologies that are bursting through the complacency of "mature" industries. American companies were scurrying in the early 1980s to respond by changing their management emphasis.

This time around knowledge of the human factors will have to be a major ingredient of top management's orientation. Coming full circle will not simply put us back to where we once were. Effective management will have added a new dimension. Technological strengths will be matched with people skills in each management team. The solution to America's quality and productivity problems lies not in shifting from one set of hard factors to another—from the analytical thinking of accountants to the analytical thinking of engineers—but in a balancing of "hard- and soft-factor" abilities.

Many managers still regard people with their values, aspirations, motivations, relationships, and other intangibles as soft factors. Sales, return on investment, price-to-earnings ratios, cost per unit—these were the hard subjects of the 1960s and 1970s. Computers, robots, complex machining centers could be the hard subjects of technology-oriented managers. But the wisdom of the 1980s and 1990s will have to be quite different. The soft stuff will become the hard stuff of management. The quantitative considerations will not be abandoned, but they will be put into better balance with qualitative factors.

This time around, we will be looking for top management who can combine operations background with the ability to view the human factors within and outside the corporation and fashion a living strategy. The development of corporate strategy, as we have known it in recent decades, has been largely in the hands of specialists and a few people in top management. It has been a strategy only in the sense that it sets some intended objectives; it does not get to the heart of the business and does not involve the people who have to implement it. Rather than reflecting the dreams of the entire organization, this sort of strategy is merely the pipe dream of a few. That's why it generally fails to be the driving force of the organization. If people don't share common objectives and values, they cannot implement a strategy. They can't begin to explore their common ground if stategy is confined to a three-ring binder for only a few to see. Many executives admit that when they look back at what their company has attained, it was not the result of any formal strategy. Frankly, many companies do not really have a strategy.

Building a New Culture

Lessons from the best companies here and abroad suggest that the best strategies are not something to be decreed by a few but a feeling or commitment that is shared by all and serves as a guide for their daily activity. These companies are more noted for their culture or shared values than for their formal strategies. In too many companies, strategy setting has been an attempt to define the big picture, but the picture has been too small. It has failed to rise to human scale, dealing only with numbers that are of little gut-level importance to people in the organization. Sometimes management has tried to create excitement in other ways that are quite removed from the product itself. Distortion of the corporate role cascades from the top, with executives inventing images that overglamorize their companies. Steel or plastics producers become "materials companies," coal miners and oil drillers become "energy companies," and office-machine producers see themselves in the "knowledge business." A grand image of the company can help avoid harboring too narrow a perception of what the company does, but the old realities of delivering specific products and services cannot be taken for granted.

In the coming years, American executives will be less concerned with strategic planning, and they will be seeking ways to demonstrate skills in *strategic management*. They will work to get their organizations to discover and define values that are shared by the members, establish a purpose that would express these values in action, and determine the specific actions necessary to proceed toward that purpose.

Each echelon of the organization should be concerned with decreasingly smaller details of the corporation's big picture, but what we find in many companies is each department and each echelon devising a picture of its own. Few companies have established mechanisms or permitted opportunities for information to flow horizontally and pull the picture together. Many managers in the middle ranks are unhappy with their role because they have a limited view of the big picture and little voice in shaping it. They are not part of the creation or execution of strategy.

Even executives who pride themselves on having an "open door policy" may hold all critical decisions and the overview of the operation to themselves. Although anyone in the company may honestly feel free to walk into the president's office at any time, the freedom to communicate with one's peers is what really counts in being well-informed and able to implement strategy. If people are serving only their bosses and are restricted in their contact with others in the company, they cannot deal directly with the continual flow of problems they cause one another. The department head who says, "Don't bother my people; you can come directly to me at any time," limits the effectiveness of his or her subordinates and those on the other side of the departmental wall.

Because people are taking an expanded view of what it means to be human, they will continually ask to what end they are working. This means the manager has to help them find a sense of purpose in their work. American corporations now need leaders who can establish purpose for their organizations that meshes with the purpose that people are struggling to work out in their personal lives. This new challenge calls for strategic thinking on a plane high above the usual "corporate strategy" or "long-range planning." Management is being called upon to elicit from people what they believe, where they want to go, and what they will commit themselves to. They are in the values business, like it or not. People's concept of what it means to be human determines the products and services they demand and the types of work and work relationships they will engage in. Unless management can deal with the human dimension as well as master the fields of technology, it will be fighting a losing battle to preserve the status quo.

It's much too simplistic to think of the restructuring of U.S. business in terms of those industries or products whose time has come and others whose time has passed. Each organization's success or failure depends on whether it puts itself into a maintenance mode or a development mode which offers a healthy environment for people to grow. A company's ability to endure depends on its ability to determine what people consider of value and then deliver the appropriate balance of quality and price. In turn, that depends not only on current technological capability but on the ability to continue innovating.

Seeing People as Unfinished Products

The fundamental determinant of an organization's health, then, is its view of people. The corporation that sees people as finished products—for better or for worse—will suffer the pains of change. The organization that regards people as capable and worthy of growth will be in tune with change and better able to manage it.

More and more managers are coming to believe that they have to refashion organizational structures and procedures to establish a culture that makes use of workers' quest for self-development and commitment to something outside themselves. They see the workforce as essentially active and dynamic, not passive and unchanging. They hold no illusions of creating a utopia, but they are trying to reach the 80 or 90 percent of the people in their organizations who will respond to work in forms that appeal to their higher levels of needs.

Cummins Engine Company, Inc., has long been noted for demonstrating concern for the well-being of its workers. In recent years, it has intensified its efforts to better manage its human resources, and that has led to experimentation with new forms of organization, such as plants with only three levels of pay to encompass all employees from the newest hiree to the plant manager. Ted Marston, vice president, describes some of the changes which his management team regarded as making it impossible to manage people in traditional organizations: "We saw a growing lack of concern on the part of many of our people for the excellence in what they did and how they did it. In our traditional plants we saw a lack of flexible skills and a very rigid work environment. We saw a more educated workforce unwilling to accept the ways we traditionally ran organizations. We saw the developing complexity of our organization and a need to broaden decision-making roles."

Can managers realistically expect to change a corporate culture?

Can they change the incentives and policies that work against human growth? Can they blend a knowledge of the soft subjects with the best of scientific management? Can they deal with both the intangible and the tangible? Difficult as their challenge is, managers are not being asked to do the impossible. C. William Verity led a major cultural change in a tradition-bound industry. When he took the reins of Armco Inc. in 1965, the company (then Armco Steel Corp.) was a steelmaker through and through; the culture was that of an organization dedicated to doing the same thing a little better year after year. But during his tenure as chairman, the company added other lines of business and set a course for both corporate and individual growth. In 1982, it began pursuing a "Quality Plus" program aimed at total workforce commitment to high-quality product and service. The first stage in the process dealt with winning the commitment of managers and preparing the proper corporate culture.

The companies that are doing the most outstanding job of managing their human resources and humanizing their companies are those that most of us would call "high technology" companies—Hewlett-Packard, IBM, Texas Instruments, and TRW Inc., for example. Small but fast-growing Tandem Computers Inc. is noted for requiring all employees to take a six-week sabbatical with full pay every four years. Looking ahead to the time when it will be a billion-dollar company, it has put managers through a training program to sensitize them to the cultural change that lies ahead.

There are enough good executives in place to show that staying atop such companies and mastering both the technology and the people factors is not an impossible role to fill. Jack Welsh, chairman of General Electric Company; Jim Renier, vice chairman of Honeywell Inc.; and Tom Vanderslice, president of General Telephone & Electronics Corp. are not only pursuing new styles of managing people but they are scientists in their own right. All three hold doctorates in scientific disciplines. Their style of leadership blends art, science, and *soul.*

Setting Aside
the Conventional Wisdom

In their quest for personal advancement and producing certain financial results, managers have not totally disregarded the people in their organizations. However, they are used to defining people as they would like them to be or as they think people once were. When people's behavior doesn't match what they expect, they look for techniques to modify that behavior. Douglas McGregor warned over two decades ago that managers might react superficially to people's behavior rather than modifying their own fundamental attitudes.[6] Assuming that people were essentially response mechanisms, managers used behavioral sciences to try to change behavior, but their methods of manipulation caused even more worker dissatisfaction. The corporation cannot tolerate the widening gap caused by that traditional management view of workers and the workers' changing view of themselves. For that matter, a new breed of managers—of all ages—is also caught in that gap because they *do* have new fundamental beliefs.

Management is heading toward a new state of mind—a new perception of its own role and that of the organization. It is slowly moving from seeking power to empowering others, from controlling people to enabling them to be creative. Operating in ways that unleash people's power runs counter to managers' tendency to monopolize power. As managers make a fundamental shift in values, a radical reorientation to a greater worldview will enable the corporation to treat its human resources as *resources*. It can regain some of the lost ground in product excitement, price competitiveness, and profitability. A growing nucleus of managers realizes they will have to set aside their conventional managerial "widom" before they can bring about any resurgence of American business. They know, too, that manageering their way upward is not going to assure them of organizations in which they can play out their careers.

When managers were dealing essentially with fixed technology and a closed economy, they could do well by simply maintaining the status quo. But the situation has changed. Technology is changing the economy and revitalizing sleepy industries, the economy is now open worldwide, and people won't always do what they're told to do. Business could rely on mindless workers and managers to maintain the old, but now it needs creative people to generate change. The current stage of industrialization will proceed only if it has greater involvement of the workforce at all levels. A movement toward flatter structures and greater participation would meet both the need for more creative and dynamic organizations and the needs of managers and nonmanagers for greater involvement in their work.

Autocratic management is inadequate for today's tough, global productivity race. It doesn't provide the best strategies, generate enough innovation, attain high enough quality in its product, or make the smartest cost reductions. If managers look only to the techniques of participative management, their thinly disguised autocratic approach will only worsen the situation. If they do not buy the underlying philosophy, they will still be trying to adapt people to systems rather than adapting themselves and their systems to the realities of today's people.

Managers will become more concerned about developing their people because it makes good business sense and it is a vital end in itself. They are in a position to point the way to small victories in people's struggle between present conditions and what they are convinced they might be. As they experiment with ways to let their more optimistic view of people guide their actions, they will see worker attitudes improve. People tend to become what they are told they are. Feedback affects their behavior and, in turn, shapes their attitudes. As Frederick Herzberg has pointed out: "Attitudes do not lead to behavior. It is rather the other way around. Behavior leads to attitudes."[7]

The manager who sets out to change an organization's culture has to deal with more than structures and procedures because the values in place in society set certain expectations of what people do as workers and managers. One evening, during an informal roundtable discussion, several executives were discussing the current clash between the values that managers might like to express and what is expected of them. Dale MacDonald, president of Na-Churs Plant Food Co., pointed out that people used to grow up learning at mother's knee that it was okay to love people, to show concern for them. But in the postwar years, we have gotten away from that, he said. "We fell out of love with people. It wasn't socially acceptable. It was a little queer. It takes a real leader to overcome that." To reverse the macho, scientific mentality imposed from within and from outside the corporation is not easy. Yet, the changing values shared by more and more managers and nonmanagers are making it more acceptable to try.

Creating Winners

Managers who conduct themselves as leaders and enablers will lead people toward personal fulfillment. They can provide small, incremental learning steps so people can feel themselves coming alive on the job—something many never dreamed was possible. This could be the dawning of a great new era—a great leap upward in people's view of themselves and the world they live in. The manager can lift people's sights and engage with them in one-on-one development. He or she has an opportunity to set goals with others and provide the working conditions, training, and relationships necessary to perform meaningful work. Some managers see their responsibility as that of leading others in becoming responsible individuals. They like to overturn the old saying "A manager gets work done through people" to "A manager gets people done through work."

Managers will increasingly find that the only way they can be winners is to create winners. There are already signs that young people today are less interested in "getting to the top." We can hope, then, that they will be more responsive to meaningful jobs in the middle ranks and that their dissatisfaction with institutions will stimulate positive changes. Managers, too, are frustrated by systems and the sacrifice of excellence for short-term financial gain. They have seen products that they created become stripped of quality, organizations lose effectiveness and efficiency, prices rise to offset declining productivity and sales volume, and customers receive less and less value.

Broader participation by the workforce will mean broader roles for all, including managers. Rather than filling the relatively narrow jobs that many of them now hold, managers will be able to test their own limits for growth by becoming leaders, enablers, consultants, and facilitators. They will have the opportunity and the need to broaden their own knowledge base and learn new skills. They will be challenged to open individuals to growth, wherever that may lead, rather than try to "peg" each individual and predict some particular level or position that person will eventually attain.

The role of the manager is becoming a transformative one. As a teacher or coach, his or her fulfillment will come increasingly from helping others find fulfillment. Managerial effectiveness, then, depends more upon setting a learning environment than a telling environment. The quality of management is determined by its ability to bring together the best efforts of the entire organization. The most effective managers are not the masters of great systems. In fact, they are somewhat the opposite. In quite unsystematic ways, they stroll through the organization, trolling for information, asking questions, encouraging people to pursue their own ideas, revealing their enthusiasm and commitment to improvement. One metal-fabricating company president, who is called a "gadfly" by his subordinates, constantly chats with his people as he makes his "rounds," prodding them to consider new ways of doing things, leaving them with questions or challenges. One young manager in the company says, "He enjoys listening to tomorrow's opportunities, not yesterday's problems. And he finds the positive things going on. He has a 'good news syndrome.' He doesn't have all the answers, but he asks a lot of the right questions."

More and more courses and experiences aimed at helping managers better understand people and develop their interpersonal skills are being added to company training programs. They are helping managers learn to be better listeners and better speakers. This increases the effectiveness of those who already have positive attitudes toward people and encourages those with negative views to modify their attitudes as they see the improved business results that can be achieved by taking the limits off people. In the past, companies sought managers who had all the right answers. Today, they need managers who can ask the right questions and elicit good ideas from the workforce.

Under these changing circumstances, the manager will no longer have to pretend to offer some sort of lifetime employment scheme. Such guarantees are impossible to execute since the manager cannot guarantee the company will exist through an employee's lifetime. He can come closer to giving people long-term employment by engaging in good manpower planning and intensive people development. The person who has begun the quest for growth and is developing technical and interpersonal skills builds job security by becoming flexible and more able to deal with technological and organizational change. Attempted guarantees, on the other hand, make people dependent rather than self-reliant.

Managers who appreciate the advantages of a participative organization and see the need to improve quality and productivity through worker commitment are sometimes anxious about their ability to effect change quickly enough to head off the competitive threats to their companies. Leading people to self-development, developing a sense of responsibility, and nurturing the technical and interpersonal skills that are needed in effective organizations do not happen quickly. But total change is not a prerequisite for building worker commitment. The transformation process doesn't have to be completed before commitment begins. In fact, the process is endless; it is never completed because people are never "finished." When managers show that they are genuinely committed to the quality of workers' lives and the quality of the organization, however, people respond positively. They can sense that they are valued. With whatever skills they have at the moment, with whatever information and ideas they can get their hands on, they will unlock the doors to improvement.

12

The Purpose Is Quality

MOST OF THE SEARCH FOR DEVELOPMENT, MEANING, AND PURPOSE has been conducted outside the workplace. Too few people have found high purpose in what they do at work despite their need to find significance either in the tasks they perform or in being part of a group that is working toward some meaningful purpose.

Not all business corporations can make their mission that of serving some lofty social purpose, but all can define some human end toward which their product or service contributes. There is no greater contribution a manager can make than to enable each worker to answer the question of what he or she is working toward.

The leader does not create purpose. He or she finds common purpose in the organization through deep self-examination and ongoing communication with others to determine what it is they want to achieve. The leader points out the direction in which all can work—toward a purpose that meets both individual and group needs. From the top to the bottom of the organization everyone acquires a sense of direction so they can "live" their corporate strategy.

Discovering Common Purpose

We mistakenly speak of leaders as being people "of vision" as though it is up to them to create and transmit a vision to others—to sell them on their own particular vision. Perhaps that is the function of a leader in certain circumstances where people will blindly follow. But in today's workplace, effective leadership depends on bringing people together in common purpose when they are aware that they are free to choose not to commit to that purpose. A leader (1) brings people's values and aspirations to the surface; (2) articulates, rather than creates, the vision or purpose and strives to enable people to work toward it; and (3) clears away the clutter so they can see the difference between what conditions are and what people are convinced they can be.

I have asked executives how they "resolve" values differences when trying to fashion a common purpose. As a rule, they say they have found that when people really get down to basics, they have no trouble reaching agreement. Their experience has taught me a new meaning for the term "common sense." When people genuinely seek what is best for the group, there does seem to be a common sense of what is of value lying beneath selfish demands or poorly informed opinions. Although individuals may differ in tastes and in the particular needs they may each be seeking to fulfill at any point in time, there are sufficient fundamental common values from which they can find common purpose.

At the top of the organization, management must help people clarify their purpose. Each echelon then should be concerned with decreasingly smaller details of that overview. Since people come in varying capacities in terms of mental powers, education, experience, and access to information, an organization must be structured so that individuals can deal with pieces of the big picture that are of appropriate size and shape. Each person should be permitted to manage as large a piece as he or she is capable of and see how it relates to the whole.

If management expresses objectives only in numerical or financial terms as though that is the ultimate end to be served, it conveys no values to which people can fully commit themselves. It then needs to implement systems to force people to sacrifice their human aspirations for short-term objectives. Then, however, the organization is working against human growth rather than capitalizing on it. When members of the organization see only financial goals as the corporate purpose, they may set only financial goals for their relationship to it. They are likely to approach work with the question "What's in it for me?" In fact, a series of questions may play over and over again as they face the demands of work:

"Why should we improve corporate profits?"

"To serve the stockholder? Why?"

"To help top management meets its goals? Why?"

"If this is strictly a financial game, what's in it for me? Better pay?"

"Then shouldn't I fight for a bigger share of the pie since money is all I'm getting out of this job?"

Management fights an uphill battle when it tries to build a feeling of unity and mutual dependence while confining corporate purpose to economic objectives. Unless the organization's members can envision some human, nonquantifiable values and purpose, they feel they are selling themselves out by committing to the corporate goals. They want something more enduring—more fulfilling to their full range of human needs.

Quality as a Way of Life

Discussing man's noble side which makes him capable of great acts, Ernest Becker pointed out, "He has to feel and believe that what he is doing is truly heroic, timeless, and supremely meaningful."[1] The corporation must set for itself the overall job of seeking quality if people are going to have something to which they can attach their self-respect. Employees know when they are being asked to make or sell a product that is not of good quality. If a corporation's objective is to deliver a low-price product, it should try to persuade neither its employees nor its customers that this is the world's finest. Its quality objective is to serve the low end of the market—to provide the best that people can obtain when they can't afford the very best. Employees can identify with giving someone *value* and feel good about what they are doing.

Self-respect or self-esteem must have an ethical basis. When that basis does not exist, people have to be manipulated into working, but when the company cares, employees will care. When they perceive the company as being unfair to them or others, they will not respond with responsible work behavior. Workers in "don't-care" companies don't mind calling in sick since they feel their absence won't hurt the system; in fact, they may be happy if it does. People who are participating in a humanistic setting, on the other hand, realize the burden they put on fellow workers and the possible economic harm their absence will cause. They realize, too, that they are undermining the respect that others have paid them. Their decision to come to work or stay home becomes an ethical one. It then becomes not simply a matter of being fired for unsatisfactory conduct but the possible pain of no longer being part of things. The humanistic organization, there-fore, runs on ethical behavior because it begins with individuals' respect for themselves, their colleagues, and others they serve. Ethics, not rule books, set the standards for behavior.

When he was chief psychologist at General Motors, Delmar "Dutch" Landen said: "We have established a close link between peo-ple's perceptions of the effectiveness and quality of the organization and their own behavior."[2] A culture of quality is reinforced in one aspect of the business after another—the quality of facilities, atten-tion to product quality, the image of the company that is conveyed through advertising, relations with the community, and so forth.

Unless a corporation can get by without worker commitment, it must turn to the quest for quality—both in setting its corporate objec-tives and in setting up the means by which it pursues them. It has to give people what they perceive as good value in terms of their pro-ducing and their consuming. Managers and nonmanagers alike have to respect what the company stands for and see that they are generat-ing something of value for others. As consumers, they want quality in the goods and services they buy.

In order to improve the value given to the customer, the supplier must raise the quality, lower the cost, or both. Various trade-offs of quality and cost make for variety in the economy and serve people's varying needs. The company biased toward short-term financial gains tends to emphasize the negative; it reduces costs in an effort to improve its own return but lowers the value received by the cus-tomer. When quality is not the number one priority, neither worker nor customer has cause for allegiance.

Not Another Numbers Game

In recent years, as the clamor arose over quality, some managers established systems to control it. But managers down the line had long been taught that top management's quest is essentially for a cheaper way of doing things—not a better way, not a better product. Their bonuses are based on trimming costs from a product, not on delivering the best product in the industry.

Management had been far removed from the heart of the busi-ness and could not articulate its new objectives effectively (if it had really changed them) or point the way by which people could attain them. It therefore had to attempt to quantify quality and impose con-trols that would push people toward meeting those standards. In many cases, this became just one more numbers game. But all the old practices and incentives—the old numbers games—worked against quality improvement. Even with the numbers, a certain percentage of one's output was expected to be of poor quality. "During the past two decades, an insidious attitude I call the 'Let-it-go Syndrome' developed," says John Flanagan, president of the Boston Gear unit of Incom International. "During this time, it became an accepted 'fact' that a certain amount of product would be defective."

If quality is part of the corporate purpose—and it should be—top management has to constantly reiterate this to the organization and continually ensure that assignments, procedures, and rewards serve the objectives that mark the way to quality improvement. The attainment of quality is more than a scheme; it is a way of life—a culture. It is not enough for management to establish systems and incentives to lower rejects or customer complaints. They must go beyond regarding quality as a necessary evil to be competitive. They must embrace quality for its own sake and win others to the same cause. Then, when it becomes ingrained in people's daily thoughts and actions, it cannot easily be subverted. Management may toss aside elaborate written strategies or objectives when the right opportunity for quick gains or unfavorable business conditions come along, but it cannot easily stray from following an unwritten culture that is built into the fabric of the organization.

Flexibility for Quality

United States business will not solve its productivity and quality problems through controls and tight work packages. A minimum of structure has to be balanced with creativity and flexibility because technological innovation and economic progress are restricted when human ingenuity and initiative are controlled out or boxed in. A company needs to improve its system continuously, but if the system in place does not relate to the quality of the product, the company cannot expect workers to deliver quality. If it limits the human factors rather than expands and capitalizes on them, people will beat the system from within. They will turn their talents to negative activities.

Quality begins with self-respect, which enables people to respect others in the organization and those whom the organization serves. For too many people, however, going to work means submitting to what someone else wants them to do. Someone else will assign the tasks, the place, the time, perhaps dictate what to wear, to whom they may speak, and perhaps when they can go to the restroom. For them, work entails the loss of freedom and self-respect. When systems steal people's self-respect, they leave no base on which to build quality.

Improvement of quality depends on a positive approach—seeking what can be added to the product or service. Unfortunately, American management has, too often, developed a negative bias and expressed it through its policies and procedures. To a large extent, the growing body of management knowledge has to do with cost reduction, manpower reduction, risk minimization, and controlling people's behavior. Its basic message is: "Thou shalt not."

In the earlier stages of industrialization, systems and structures were directed at creating uniformity of product and work without regard for workers' self-respect. They led to products that were, on average, of good quality. Systems rewarded people for their sameness rather than helping them develop their unique skills and set high personal goals. Today, people want to be recognized for their individuality. When they aren't, they work against the system, and quality deteriorates. Old-style systems and structures don't reinforce the newer, high-discretion types of work which call for highly skilled people who can manage themselves and adapt to unforeseen problems and opportunities.

Tight control is no substitute for individual initiative in many work situations. Even in fairly routine work that is tied closely to machines or a fast-paced series of tasks, an individual can spot trouble or potential trouble–causing developments. If workers are permitted little or no flexibility, they cannot inject their human judgment; they fall short in their quality of service to the customer or others in the same organization who depend on their work. Where the work routine is less rigid and workers have more discretion as to how to invest their time, it is more obvious that self-respect and positive attitudes play a substantial part in the quality of service.

Autocratic management can control out a great deal of people's bad behavior, but it cannot control in all the infinite details that make for quality work. That can come only from committed, competent people who are constantly searching for ways to do their jobs better. Managers like to think of themselves as agents of change—as people who manage change. But they fool only themselves if they think their systems and controls can bring positive change. Leaders, however, give people the resources and environment in which *they* can find the route to change and improvement *for themselves*. A powerful leader points the way to the infinite—toward excellence which continually moves away as one approaches it. He seeks excellence in serving the corporate purpose, whatever the product or service may be. He causes people to continually raise their standards, using attained objectives as the springboard to still greater excellence.

In the coming years, the corporation will enhance its effectiveness to the degree that it reduces its controls and downward negative messages about what people cannot do and improves the upward flow of positive messages. Rather than determining "here's what you can't do," management will elicit people's ideas about "what we can do." Effective managers see the unlimited potential in human power and place no bounds on their organizations. They are concerned with direction, with process; they do not limit their attention to attainment of a specific objective along the way. They develop organizations that can set, attain, and then set new objectives.

As management begins responding to the need to build in quality, it has to win worker commitment to quality by demonstrating its own concern. It was only after Ford's Employee Involvement program was well-established that it could publicize its renewed quest for quality. It then could advertise the slogan "Quality is Job 1" with advertising copy that read "Ford Motor Company and The United Auto Workers are working together like never before. Together we are developing more efficient assembly methods, greater productivity, and better quality."

Generally, when management has revealed its dedication to quality, it has found that the workers were already there. John Flanagan says his company traced its quality problems and found that 85 percent of them were due to shortcomings of management, not the workers. "We have found that the worker was performing optimally in terms of the judgment and skill he brought to bear on his product, but the tools—the machines he used—were not being maintained well enough to give reliable and consistent results." He found, for example, that machinists compensated for the unreliability of their machines by setting them in ways that would leave too much metal on a workpiece rather than erring on the low side. This permitted the pieces to be reworked, if necessary.

Meeting Uncertainty Head-On

When a manager nurtures self-reliance in others and taps the creativity and commitment of his workforce, he or she no longer has to waste energy trying to maintain a pretense of knowing it all. Today, no one individual can know the business, the product, and the production–distribution processes thoroughly enough to direct every detail throughout the organization. The challenge to the manager is not to learn all that a person would have to know to attend to all the right considerations and make all the right decisions. It's a tougher one than that. It requires the willingness to stand before all the members of the organization and share the unknowns, reveal a commitment to some ultimate values and purpose, and then share the collected wisdom of the workforce in order to translate those values into purposeful action. It calls for the courage to say: "Here are the realities—the competitive situation. We've got some problems. Who has some ideas for solving them?" It depends on being trustful enough to make available detailed information so workers can understand the problems and the costs and benefits related to the ideas they might offer.

An excellent manager is characterized more by a dedication to keeping the grand vision alive than by the mastery of detail. That requires the ability to synthesize and find order in complex situations so the vision is not lost. If any single tool would typify the excellent manager, it would be the wide brush of an artist, not a computer. Enlightened workers do not expect their managers to have all the right answers. They appreciate one who is genuinely posing questions in a way that invites them to grow and participate in the business. They appreciate a manager who is striving for something of value and sees them as valuable beings.

Admittedly, this represents a major break with tradition. American managers, especially, have seen themselves as people who can define any problem and solve it. In other cultures, however, people are more apt to realize that life presents many situations, some of which can be modified and some of which have to be endured. Not everything can be clearly defined as a problem with a clearly correct solution, however. People realize that life is complex. Simple problems and simple solutions are merely illusions; belief in them does not produce quality results. Enlightened people are likely to regard a leader more highly for the intensity of his or her search for the truth than for any claims of knowing the whole truth. The manager who wants to help others grow and lead them to quality performance must have the courage to meet uncertainty head on.

People want to know where their leader is coming from and where that person is going. They must see how the leader's values mesh with those of the organization so they can know how their own values relate to it. Without shared values, they cannot "track" where the organization is headed or anticipate how their individual actions may or may not contribute to the corporate purpose. That is why a person's "value dimension" will be increasingly important in his or her consideration for supervisory or management positions. More than ever before, the manager must shape and clarify the values of the organization, not in the sense of propagandizing, but by sharing convictions and doubts. The selection of managers, therefore, will have to take into consideration the ability of an individual to engage in values discussion more than in the past.

The person who would adopt a humanistic management style has to first reveal that he or she is human—not perfect but working toward improvement. This is not an easy proposition for managers already in place, working by the old standards and expectations. Some will make the switch in style to join those who are already "there" to lead the organizations of the future. They will rely on anyone in the organization who can make a contribution to quality. They will strip away some of the rigidity from their systems. Through character, rather than control, they will define and pursue the corporate purpose.

Both character and quality are based on truth. A person's character is revealed in his or her dedication to all the aspects of quality: the product or service itself, the production and distribution processes and their impact on the environment, the worklife of those associated with the product, and the social impact of the product in its usage. If a manager is concerned only about the quality of the product and ignores the quality of the workers' lives or the impact of his business on the environment, he is trying to segment quality. But quality cannot be segmented. In his futile effort, he segments himself and his stakeholders. Any attempt to attain only one narrow measure of quality falls short in giving the manager and his workers something of meaning to which they can be committed.

Character has to do with one's search for wholeness, for consistency, for truth, for excellence. Quality of product or service is determined by individuals who can hold out a vision of what can be and then enable others to work toward it. The ability to do that is, in turn, the fundamental measure of the quality of management.

American management faces not so much a test of skills as a test of character. Success in meeting that test will go well beyond the resultant economic gains to the progress people can make in terms of self-fulfillment and meaningful lives.

13

The Soul of Management

THE MANAGER'S ABILITY TO CONTRIBUTE TO HUMAN DEVELOPMENT and create viable organizations in today's values environment will depend on two things that are far more important than the technical skills he or she may have. First is the matter of what the manager believes—what his or her worldview is. Second is the degree to which the manager will employ a management style that expresses these beliefs.

An increasing number of managers are revealing that they hold the basic philosophy needed to support their operating in a genuinely humanistic and participative manner. They take an optimistic view of people. They are learning to practice what I have termed "humanagement."[1] They are managers who:

1. Regard people as a whole persons—as individuals. They reveal this in the way they deal with workers, customers, suppliers, and the public
2. Help people invest more of themselves in their work and derive meaning and personal growth from it
3. Recognize the importance of people's relationships within organizations beyond those spelled out in the organization charts
4. Take an optimistic view of people and create organizations that foster cooperation
5. Reveal their own fears, weaknesses, aspirations, and soul

Managers do have soul! They are interested in the transcendental connection. They attend church, read the Bible, and pray. As a group, they are at least as moral and religious as the general public.[2] One detailed study of American values shows that business leaders closely parallel the public in expressing moral concern over such matters as adultery, abortion, premarital sex, homosexuality, use of marijuana and hard drugs, and pornographic movies. Leaders in sectors that we might think of as more responsible for our moral direction—in the news media, education, and government—are less likely than business leaders or the public to consider these matters moral issues.

The spirituality of business management comes through equally clear. Aside from religious leaders, business executives rank highest among leadership groups in various expressions of religious commitment; they most closely resemble the general public and stand well ahead of leaders in the news media, voluntary associations, the military, government, law, education, and science. Business executives actually outdo the public when it comes to saying they frequently encourage others to turn to religion, attend religious services, and engage in prayer.[3]

No survey should be needed to affirm the commitment of managers to church and community activities. All we have to do is look around us to see them at work outside the workplace. This involvement in itself does not necessarily prove these people have spiritual commitment or awareness, however. Some of them could be seeking outlets for their skills and energy; and so I have asked manager after manager what they credit for their effectiveness in dealing with people humanistically and for their positive outlook on life. Many mention such things as "The Good Book," or "my Southern Baptist upbringing," or some other experience that oriented them along the transcendental axis. Some are operating simply from a base of humanism which does not concern itself with a supreme creator; but they believe people are improvable and definitely worth improving.

People with this deeper sense of purpose and greater sense of man's worth tend to become the successful leaders. They are willing to take risks for what they believe, they are not afraid to seek the help of others, and they have the ability to inspire others to join in their quest. These are the outstanding entrepreneurs, corporate statesmen, and managers in the middle who battle the traditional hierarchy. People with commitment to values that transcend the economic ones are those who have proven best at setting out a vision that inspires good economic performance as a by-product of serving some human purpose.

As more and more people work toward self-development and self-actualization, they will explore the ethical and spiritual considerations of life. Personal growth inevitably leads to questions of who one is and why one exists. It leads to questions beyond the self. Members of an organization will expect their leaders to be engaged in the same questioning—perhaps be a little ahead of them. They do not expect someone to erase all life's problems and questions, but they are at work either to master life or to mask the awesomeness of what it means to be plunged into a life they cannot fully control. They welcome the opportunity to test their talents in the marketplace and work toward a meaningful corporate purpose.

People are not looking for spiritual leaders in the workplace, but they are more likely to follow leaders who are spiritual—who have some deep sense of purpose that transcends the material factors of the business. It is not the role of the manager to advocate a particular set of religious beliefs, but revealing that he is in search of meaning can heighten his effectiveness. Also, he must conduct himself in such a way that shows he respects the diversity of such pursuits in others. In other words, the manager must convey the message: "I respect you as a human being in all your dimensions and that includes the transcendental."

The Too-Tight
Management Culture

By and large, American managers have created a culture of management that is far too narrow to win the dedication of their workers. Their culture does not even fit their own inner beliefs in many cases. No matter how moral, religious, or humanistic managers may be at heart, they often do not empathize with the inner feelings of others. They do not allow their inner vision to affect the way they conduct themselves at work.

The closest the typical manager comes to expressing an ideology relating to business is something he calls "free enterprise." Too often, the manager espousing free enterprise seems to be advocating some sort of negative ideology, however. It's a me-oriented position centered on a "leave-me-alone" attitude—taken, perhaps, to serve his own narcissism. What he or she *doesn't* believe is that government should interfere with business organizations. Quite often, campaigners for free enterprise are perceived by others as being linked with a negative view of people and society.

Business executives find it difficult to promote free enterprise among their own employees because they have not permitted them to be free or enterprising. Too often, they demand the freedom to make commitments that can have major impact on resources and markets and, yet, they tightly define what workers can do, where they will do it, and when. They want rewards for the bold and innovative, yet they expect their workers to be compliant. Free enterprise has become the system for the corporation or key executives but not for most of the corporation's employees.

Defenders of free enterprise have little success in selling the concept even to those who have benefited from the wealth it has generated because the battle for free enterprise has to be fought on different grounds. It has to be sold on something more than the economic facts. Its proponents have to show that the system gives people choices for a better life in more than material terms—that it is a means to human ends, not an end in itself. "Free enterprise" produces neither freedom nor effective enterprise unless it is employed as a means to serving everyone. It is not a special status for the business corporation but a basic need of all individuals. Each person must be free to earn a livelihood and to contribute to the good of the community by developing his or her uniqueness.

Free enterprise can be practiced effectively only by people who can balance freedom and responsibility. They must be free enough to be whole persons who can behave responsibly. As the momentum builds for orienting the corporation into better alignment with human values, therefore, the sellers of free enterprise will find they have a growing number of allies. When employees believe management is dedicated to human growth, when they see that free enterprise is part of being fully human, and when they can participate in it, they will support it—in fact, clamor for it.

Failure to Respond

There are many reasons why management does not respond to people's need for esteem and growth. Some are simply not interested; they lack a set of values that includes a concern for developing others. But perhaps far more are blocked by conventions that get in the way of acting out their beliefs at work. In the first place, corporate policy, corporate objectives, and standards of performance direct their attention away from problems to which they would like to apply corporate action. Secondly, some managers agonize over the gap between what they feel they are permitted to do within the confines of corporate activity and what they believe they should be doing. Although they are ready to respond to human needs, they are hesitant to make the first move in their organizations that have suppressed any expression of values beyond those set down in "business" terms. Some—even at high levels of management—are, quite frankly, afraid of being fired.

"I'm a prisoner in my own corporation," one executive confided to a small group of us who were gathered for three days to discuss ways to bring corporate resources to bear on the world's human problems. He was deeply troubled by worldwide hunger, unemployment, and pollution, but he was convinced that it would be career suicide to express these views to the top management of his company—especially to reveal the religious base for his position.

Hesitancy to put one's beliefs into gear at work is due not only to expectations or restrictions imposed from inside the corporation. Society has insisted that the corporation not intrude on individuals' values, morality, or religious beliefs. This has discouraged managers from expressing their own values and beliefs and contributed to their advancing a values-free, scientific approach to the conduct of business.

Today, managers are not certain what society expects from them. What, for instance, does it regard as the qualities of a good leader? The public looks for "honesty" and "character" before competence in the skills required by a particular position. Leaders, by contrast, tend to play down the importance of character and feel that competence is the thing most expected of them.[4]

Perhaps this discrepancy can be explained by the public's changing expectations of what the role of a leader is. It is no longer looking for someone with all the answers—with complete competence—as it might have in simpler times. Now, people want to join with a leader of inner strength and intelligence who will search with them for the truth. Managers with the traditional concept of their role lag behind in their expectations of themselves, still trying to be master, boss, or paternal overseer.

Try as they might, some managers cannot break through to a more humanistic style even when they think they are doing so. For example, a number of times, after I have spoken to groups of businessmen about participative management and serving the many levels of people's needs, some manager has come forward to tell me how much my remarks have helped him change his thinking. Then, he says he is going to set to work right away to implement a profit sharing or some other bonus system in his company. Such people are missing the underlying philosophy and are clinging, with the best of paternalistic intentions, to a narrow economic view of their employees.

Most managers are fairly decent to people. They seem to fit neither the Theory X nor Theory Y patterns. They are not especially negative in their view of people, yet they do not help people grow and become more self-reliant. Those who are concerned primarily about their own security or advancement are generally no more negative in their relations with others than they have to be to get what they want.

Even managers with strong religious and social convictions do not always see themselves as responsible for the development of others. Because management has relied on the repression of the need for human growth and fulfillment in the past, today's managers understandably are not fully aware of the discrepancy between their beliefs and their actions. If they are aware of this contradiction, they may figure that nothing can be done about it. In addition, not all religious beliefs foster a positive view of people. Some religions, in fact, teach of the fundamental evil of man. Others, at best, advocate that leaders assume a paternalistic role.

The Weakness
in Management Education

Unfortunately, the education of most managers has not contributed to their appreciation of the nobility of humanity or their regard for workers as more than a business cost. In the university and especially in the business school, their studies concentrate on quantitative methods and the hard factors of business. As a result, we find a management cadre that is more comfortable with the precision of numbers than the imprecision of people. Differences in values, interests, abilities, and modes of thinking do not, however, lend themselves to scientific analysis and rational planning.

The thing most lacking in the education of our leaders, says Michael Maccoby, is "education in the humanities." He sees shortcomings not only in writing and speaking abilities but in terms of understanding religion, philosophy, psychology, and history.[5] Dr. Albert Kaltenthaler, managing director of West Germany's Rosenthal A. G., once commented to me that, early in his career, he assumed that his business education was essentially the same as that of his American

counterparts. However, he now realizes that "we learned more about
human beings in school. We had a broad cultural education. We
studied other languages and other cultures."

The history of man's development and the great teaching of the
world's religions are all we have to guide us in life, says Frederick
Herzberg. "Literature is one of the human products that can teach us
most about people."[6] Lon Sheely, president of Star Manufacturing
Company, believes, "You can get an understanding of people out of
classic literature." He set himself a goal of reading 150 books in a ten-
year period. In his ninth year at it—which was when he told me this—
he was paying a retired actress to read books into a tape recorder. He
then played the cassettes in his car while traveling to and from work
and even while crouching in a duck blind on vacation.

It wasn't until I was well into my first university teaching experience that I was fully convinced that the humanities can help lay the
foundation for leadership. I had agreed to teach a course on "Manpower Problems" for which the textbook was essentially an
economist's view of employment, unemployment, welfare, and training programs. It dealt with some of man's most troublesome problems
but only in terms of statistics, legislation, and judicial decisions; and
so, three weeks into the course, I assigned the reading of "Death of a
Salesman." These upperclassmen and candidates for masters of business administration degrees had been geared to courses in account-
ing, business analysis, and economics. I was gambling that when the
appointed evening arrived half of the class might show up. (And I was
painfully certain that none of them would have read the play.) The
evening arrived. Thirty out of thirty-one students were present. As
our discussion sped along for two hours, I could detect no one who
had not done the reading. Nearly everyone made some observation
that taught me something about the play that I had not seen in my
own reading of it.

From that night on, we referred again and again to Willy Loman
and his family as we studied the problems of employment, unemployment, and underemployment. As we examined government programs, economic policies, and management practices, we frequently
looked back to this "real life" character. We found no easy answers to
"manpower problems," but we were able to set numbers, programs,
and techniques against the soft realities of man that had come across
through this reading assignment. Why was Willy no longer a successful salesman? Who was responsible for his becoming ineffective?
What does it feel like to fail in your profession?

Our class had learned something about character—about people's weaknesses and strengths—about their determination to triumph over reality or, if need be, reject it as Willy did. We had observed people as they are and as they hope to be. The purpose of studying the humanities is not to find simple solutions to management problems. It is to understand or at least become aware of some of life's fundamental problems and situations. It is to raise questions rather than to present answers.

Education for managers of the future must include far more than the teaching of techniques for reducing all situations to problems for which there are clear solutions. Greater exposure to dilemmas would raise appreciation for the struggle in people's lives and lower managers' eagerness to press for simple solutions which deny things that are important to people. A manager's effectiveness depends on the ability to resolve conflict, live with ambiguity, and face up to the indefinite and even the infinite.

In the early 1980s, many business schools underwent a great deal of soul-searching to determine how they could bring some of the human resource factors into their curricula. Unfortunately, they were looking for appropriate injections of courses on managing people; they were not looking at a fundamentally different orientation from the strictly analytical one. Ethics and values cannot be taught in courses on ethics and values. Even total immersion in the humanities cannot ensure the development of sensitivity to people and the courage to do something to alleviate their problems. No particular degree or formal curriculum qualifies one as a manager because management is increasingly becoming a matter of character.

Personal Values—
A Public Concern

Tradition, expectations of others, and outright fear all weigh against managers' revealing the positive aspects of their character. For decades, the building of great economic organizations called for denial of the manager's own soul. But the strictly economic approach to managing is straining against the limits of its effectiveness. In the future, managers will be immersed in human and transcendental issues. They will need the assurance of their own values and an appreciation of those of other people whether they are similar or different from their own. They will have to share their values and encourage others to do likewise.

In 1979, I asked C. Peter McColough, then chairman of Xerox Corporation, what he thought the essential traits of the chief executive officers of our future corporations should be. He said that, in light of all the deep concerns expressed by people, he could not see "how you can really lead people without clearly showing that you've got some concern for these broad problems—that you have integrity, that you have personal values that are important to you and, therefore, to the institution."[7]

At that same time, David Roderick, who was chairman of United States Steel Corporation, suggested that management may have to reveal its soul. The public will no longer accept a chief executive who ia "a nameless and faceless guy running a business that affects the community. The public wants to know who he is, what he stands for, what he looks like, whether he is a decent guy, whether he can be relied on."[8] Up to now, values have had little place in the workplace. But in an era of changing and sometimes conflicting values, management will have to resolve these issues, or, at least, bring them into a state of equilibrium. Not all conflicts will be neatly resolved.

Michael Maccoby, in his popular 1976 book, *The Gamesman*, portrayed the successful manager as one who denied his own humanity and that of others in order to build winning teams. (Not that Maccoby advocated such career strategy.) In his 1981 book, *The Leader*, Maccoby called for far more human qualities in managers, however: "In the eighties, the gamesman's style no longer works. The leader is unable to succeed by playing people off against each other. Faced with the need to compromise and sacrifice, unless there are shared ideals and trust, each person plays for himself at the expense of others."[9]

Changing from Within

Negative perceptions of managers have led many people to insist that any change in the nature of the corporation will have to come from without, but a substantial amount of meaningful change has been coming from within. Necessity for change is emanating from inside managers since many of them find it difficult to refrain from expressing their own values. Business executives are well out in front when it comes to sensing and nurturing the new values and the possibilities for what individuals may become. They are convinced that the economic definition of man is too confining for themselves and others. Marilyn Ferguson agrees, "Increasing numbers of business leaders are trying to articulate a new perspective." In fact, she says, "business executives may be the most open-minded group in society . . . because their success depends on their being able to perceive early trends and new perspectives."[10]

While numerous pressure groups are making their conflicting demands on the corporation, it is corporate leadership that will hammer out a new mission that meets both economic and noneconomic needs within the bounds of reality. Top management is spearheading the movement to open corporate doors for human growth. In general, it seems to be more optimistic than the general public about people's potential. The Roper Organization, after studying fifty chief executive officers, concluded that this group was stronger than the general public in faith in the future, confidence in youth, and belief in American workers. For example, only 14 percent of these corporate officers said they believed that American workers don't work as hard as workers in other countries while 36 percent of the public held that view.[11]

People entering the management ranks are likely to be those who are seeking self-actualization because they perceive management positions as the best places in which to exercise what they have learned and to encounter new learning experiences. Maslow believed that self-actualizing people are the most compassionate people and the best fighters against injustice and for excellence.[12] The manager who is self-actualizing is likely to strive to tailor organizations to fit people while the manager who is seeking his own gratification on lower levels of need tries to make people fit organizations.

It is well-known that many jobs have been "Taylorized"—broken down into simple tasks—at the lower levels. We may not appreciate how much managers' jobs have been similarly limited. From its very beginning, the role of the hired manager was one of specialization. Managerial jobs can be narrow and dull. Many managers as well as nonmanagers want to bring more to the job and take more from it. They, too, are concerned with personal growth.

Today's manager lives in the midst of the new ethical milieu. As more and more managers embrace the emerging paradigm and wider definition of man, they will change their expectations of how work and organizations should be structured. The corporation, therefore, will undergo evolutionary, but rapid, change for two reasons: (1) new people coming into management may have different values and priorities than their predecessors; and (2) mature managers who have long held the "new" values are now coming forth because these values are more acceptable today and they make good business sense as well.

Managment's reexamination of its own orientation began with

questioning its methods for achieving economic objectives; some of the reexamination has gone even deeper than that. Some managers question the wisdom of having regarded economics as the highest or only end for business to serve in the first place. They suspect, and the evidence is building to support them, that by first showing concern for both workers and the public, they will improve economic performance along the way.

An increasing number of executives and middle managers are convinced that they are not in an either-or situation where they must choose between human growth and economic growth. They see the humanistic approach to management as serving people on all their levels of needs—material and nonmaterial. They have seen that when management tries to serve only economic objectives, the members of the organization retaliate by seeking their own economic advantage with the resultant loss of both human and economic power.

The next breakthrough in management has already begun—not in some better form of financial analysis or organizational controls—but in the manager's better understanding of himself. Perspective—not technique—and a new vision of its own role will create an ideology of management that relates its activities to fundamental human issues. It is in the demise of past management practices and attitudes that we can find hope for rejuvenation of both the corporation and the individuals in it. Managers for whom the economic realm is part of a greater worldview will make way for themselves and others to find greater significance in their lives. The rise of a healthy ethic characterized by interest in self-development, commitment to others, and orientation toward producing will contribute substantially more to individual growth and corporate health than would the simple extension of the old ethic, which compelled people to surrender to the organization. Suppressed workers and frustrated managers will come alive when they see themselves as multidimensional creatures with unlimited potential.

14

Agenda for Management Action

THE PROCESS OF HUMANIZING THE CORPORATION IS MOVING FORWARD but not as fast as it might because misperceptions on the part of the public and the members of the corporation itself obscure what could happen and even what is now happening. The opportunity for people's coming alive at work is being unnecessarily limited by management's assumptions about people and the public's impression of what is going on in the corporation—both of which are out-of-date.

The workplace offers immeasurable potential for human growth and for attacking social and economic problems at their source. Management needs to capitalize on this potential in order to meet its economic objectives, and others need to appreciate this potential so they will not expect political contrivances that punish or protect business to get to the roots of people's failure to find fulfillment.

Members of the organization, at all levels, and the general public need to set aside outdated concepts of the corporation and set several new assumptions in their place:

1. The corporation's productivity has human dimensions beyond simple output-and-input calculations.
2. The corporation serves not just its owners but a number of stakeholders—employees, customers, suppliers, and the public.
3. The corporation bears considerable responsibility for the education of its stakeholders.

193

4. The corporation is a process—a human process—not merely a legal entity. Its primary obligation is to society for whatever purposes society chooses.
5. The corporation is involved in the ethical and moral issues surrounding it, whether it is so directed by law or not.
6. The corporation plays a major role in shaping the values of its various stakeholders, and this role is becoming increasingly positive.
7. Nurturing a producer mentality produces both a healthier economy and more human growth than does nurturing a consumer mentality.
8. Cooperation by growing persons is more effective than competition among persons crowded into narrowly defined roles.
9. Work and the work situation can be a rich source of meaning, identity, personal development, and a sense of community.
10. The corporation, led by managers who perceive the new image of man as well as the demands of the economic arena, is changing from within. Many of the corporate risk takers and innovators are in the forefront of exploring the full dimensions of humanity and the new values.

"Business is a yeasty place for change," said Marilyn Ferguson at the 1982 World Future Society assembly. Yet, the public has been slow to perceive the changes that are occurring and the potential that they suggest. It is generally unaware of the many new commitments to quality-of-life programs, quality circles, and other participative processes. It has heard little of the material riches accruing from such developments and practically nothing of the human richness pouring into workers' lives.

Management itself is not totally committed to the new assumptions about work and the workplace. Even those managers who are in the forefront of change may not know how to put their convictions and hunches into practice. They are in a central position for helping us relate to one another and develop to our full human potential; there are numerous actions that they can take to accelerate the trend toward humanization of the corporation and make those changes known to the public so it will support their efforts. To help them on their way, let us conclude our study of people coming alive at work by suggesting an agenda for management action:

1. Take stock of your fundamental beliefs—what's important in your life—as well as any doubts that are important.
2. View your role and that of your organization in the largest possible context.
3. Continually assess the values of your organization's various stakeholder groups.
4. Tell others in the organization where you are coming from and where you would like to go.
5. Study the values, seek the vision of your stakeholders, and then work toward building a common purpose.
6. Include employees at all levels in discussion of values issues related to what the company does and how it conducts its business.
7. Establish noneconomic as well as economic objectives for the organization, and make them widely known.
8. Set standards of excellence and make them known internally and externally.
9. Communicate purpose, values, and standards honestly and sincerely in terms that your audience can understand.
10. Invite customers and special-interest groups to discuss reactions to proposed products and production processes.
11. Explain to the public the cost, benefits, and risks of proceeding with or refraining from specific technological innovations.
12. Promote work as a rewarding and fulfilling activity.
13. Develop advertising programs that lead to a producer mentality rather than a consumer ethic.
14. Strive to develop *individuals* in your organization.
15. Make people "visible." Help them attain a feeling of significance.
16. Lead people to teamwork by helping them to realize their interdependencies and to respect the worth of others.
17. Establish corporate training and development programs to enable individuals to evaluate themselves realistically and explore their potential for growth.
18. Ensure that each job is analyzed in terms of its true educational requirements so that unnecessary barriers will not be placed in the way of otherwise qualified people.
19. Commit to continuous educational programs that will enable workers to acquire both technical skills and skills that will help them in interpersonal relationships.

20. Encourage and support the educational sector in the development of people rather than seeking training for specific, short-term needs.

21. Provide educational opportunities for employees beyond those relating directly to their present jobs.

22. Encourage all workers to participate in problem solving, doing everything you can to sustain the process once you have initiated it.

23. Work with labor representatives to reduce job classifications and create flexible, more rewarding work.

24. Bring workers, management, and labor union officials together to discuss the impact of new technology well before its introduction to determine the impact on work content and working conditions.

25. Share corporate financial information and plans—the good news and the bad—so employees at all levels will know where the organization is headed, how it is doing, and how they can contribute more effectively.

26. Enable work groups to take over their own scheduling, administrative work, analysis of equipment needs, and facilities design.

27. Support work groups when they are ready to move beyond dealing with problems relating to their primary function to a broader role inside and outside the corporation.

28. Teach consensus-building skills rather than reliance on hierarchical power and politics.

29. Structure subordinate managers' duties to allow time and resources for dealing with values issues.

30. Evaluate managers on their contribution to long-term objectives and people development.

31. Reward managers for performance on quantifiable human resource factors, such as low levels of worker grievances, low absenteeism, and development of work skills, as well as on improved quality of product and service.

32. Train managers in problem solving, communications, and leadership skills.

33. Select and promote managers who have the capacity to appreciate and deal with values issues.

34. Encourage and reward managers for participation in community, regional, and national activities through which they can become sensitized to a broad range of interests, concerns, and opportunities for contributing to human growth.

35. Provide support and education for middle managers and first-line supervisors to overcome their reluctance to share decision-making responsibility with their subordinates.
36. Enable managers and supervisors to establish networks inside and outside the company through which they can share concerns and successes in implementing participative management practices.

This agenda suggests the boundless role a manager can play in bringing excitement and fulfillment into the lives of others and into his or her own life since the achievements of the manager of tomorrow will increasingly be determined by one's ability to empower others to achieve. One manager cannot do all that needs to be done. On the other hand, every manager can do something. Top management can open the door to sweeping change, and middle managers and first-line supervisors can transmit the message of human growth and dedicate themselves to the empowering process.

Social-economic malaise is the sum of individuals' inability to meet their needs, and its cure lies in unleashing individual potential to produce solutions. Individual growth and development will come, not through a grand scheme, but through sustained, one-on-one relationships in which people enable one another to achieve.

Notes

Chapter 1
Failing One Another

1. Amitai Etzioni, *An Immodest Agenda*, McGraw-Hill Book Company, New York, 1981, pp. 3–4.
2. Christopher Lasch, *The Culture of Narcissism*, W. W. Norton & Company, Inc., New York, 1978.
3. Willis Harman, *An Incomplete Guide to the Future*, San Francisco Book Company, Inc., San Francisco, 1976, p. 120.
4. Michael Maccoby, *The Leader*, Simon & Schuster, New York, 1981, p. 49.
5. Daniel Yankelovich, *New Rules*, Random House, Inc., New York, 1981, p. 12.
6. Etzioni, op. cit., pp. 108, 131.

Chapter 2
Not by Bread Alone

1. Abraham Maslow, "A theory of motivation," *Psychological Review* 50, 1943, pp. 370–96.
2. Frederick Herzberg, Bernard Mausner, and Barbara Snyderman, *The Motivation to Work*, John Wiley & Sons, New York, 1959.
3. Ernest Becker, *The Denial of Death*, The Free Press, New York, 1973, p. 26.

4. Ibid., p. 4.

5. Frederick Herzberg, "Piecing together generations of values," *Industry Week*, October 1, 1979, pp. 58–63.

6. Daniel Yankelovich, "We need new motivational tools," *Industry Week*, August 6, 1979, pp. 61–68.

7. Daniel Yankelovich and John Immerwahr, "Putting the Work Ethic to Work," The Public Agenda Foundation, New York, September 1983.

8. "How Families Are Balancing Home, Work Responsibilities," *World of Work Report*, Work in America Institute, Scarsdale, N.Y., June 1982, pp. 44, 45.

9. Douglas McGregor, *The Human Side of Enterprise*, McGraw-Hill Book Company, New York, 1960.

10. Ernest Becker, *Escape from Evil*, The Free Press, New York, 1975, p. 31.

11. Robert Schrank, *Ten Thousand Working Days*, The MIT Press, Cambridge, Mass., 1978, p. 143.

12. Pope John Paul II, "Laborem Exercens," September 14, 1981. (Claudia Carlen, *The Papal Encyclicals 1958–81*, McGrath Publishing Co., Raleigh, N.C., 1981, pp. 301–2.)

13. Ibid., p. 299.

14. Ibid., p. 301.

Chapter 3
What Happened to the
Old Protestant Ethic?

1. "The Connecticut Mutual Life Report on American Values in the '80s," Connecticut Mutual Life Insurance Co., Hartford, Conn., 1981, p. 42.

2. "The Continental Group Report: Toward Responsible Growth," The Continental Group Inc., Stamford, Conn., 1982, p. 76.

3. Ewald M. Plass, *This is Luther*, Concordia Publishing House, St. Louis, Mo., 1948, p. 278.

4. Max Weber, *The Protestant Ethic and the Spirit of Capitalism*, Charles Scribner's Sons, New York, 1958, p. 81.

5. Jeremy Rifkin, *The Emerging Order*, G. P. Putnam's Sons, New York, 1979, p. 21.

6. Max Weber, op. cit., p. 176.

7. Daniel T. Rodgers, *The Work Ethic in Industrial America 1850–1920*, The University of Chicago Press, Chicago, 1974, p. 28.

8. Ibid., p. 9.

9. Daniel Bell, *The Cultural Contradictions of Capitalism*, Basic Books, Inc., New York, 1976, p. 59.

10. Max Weber, op. cit., 176–77.

11. Ibid., p. 182.

12. Neill Q. Hamilton, *Recovery of the Protestant Adventure*, Seabury Press, New York, 1981, p. 15.
13. Martin Marty, *Righteous Empire*, The Dial Press, New York, 1970, p. 179.
14. Max Weber, op. cit., p. 17.

Chapter 4
What Went Wrong at Work?

1. Daniel Yankelovich and John Immerwahr, "Putting the Work Ethic to Work," The Public Agenda Foundation, New York, September 1983.
2. "Workers Attitudes Toward Productivity," U.S. Chamber of Commerce, Washington, D.C. 1980, p. 11.
3. "The Connecticut Mutual Life Report on American Values in the '80s," Connecticut Mutual Life Insurance Co., Hartford, Conn., 1981, p. 159.
4. Michael Maccoby, *The Leader*, Simon and Schuster, New York, 1981, p. 53.
5. "Perspectives on Productivity: A Global View," Sentry Insurance Company, Stevens Point, Wis., 1981, p. 9.
6. Daniel Yankelovich and John Immerwahr, op. cit.
7. Peter F. Drucker, *The Changing World of the Executive*, Times Books, New York, 1982, p. 153.
8. M. R. Cooper, B. S. Morgan, P. M. Foley, and L. B. Kaplan, "Changing employee values: deepening discontent?" *Harvard Business Review*, January–February 1979, p. 124.
9. Daniel Yankelovich and John Immerwahr, op. cit.
10. "Workers' Attitudes Toward Productivity," (see note 2), pp. 12, 17.
11. Michael Maccoby, op. cit., p. 42.
12. Ibid., p. 52.
13. Ibid., p. 50.

Chapter 5
End of the Consumption Binge

1. Daniel Yankelovich, *New Rules*, Random House, New York, 1981, pp. 188–89.
2. Amitai Etzioni, "Choose America must," *Across the Board*, The Conference Board, October 1980, p. 47.
3. Peter F. Drucker, *Managing in Turbulent Times*, Harper & Row, Publishers, Inc., New York, 1980, pp. 85–86.
4. Ibid., p. 96.
5. James A. Baker, vice president of General Electric Company, speech at Milwaukee World Trade Conference, May 19, 1982.

6. "New Work Schedules to Aid Employees, Employers in '80s," *World of Work Report*, Work in America Institute, Scarsdale, N.Y., November 11, 1981, p. 81.

Chapter 6
Whirlwind of Changing Values

1. "The Continental Group Report: Toward Responsible Growth," The Continental Group Inc., Stamford, Conn., 1982, p. 20.
2. Ibid., p. 146.
3. Ibid., p. 47.
4. Jeremy Rifkin, *The Emerging Order*, G. P. Putnam's Sons, New York, 1979, p. 29.
5. Rene Dubos, *A God Within*, Charles Scribner's Sons, New York, 1972, p. 253.
6. Hans Kung, *Does God Exist?*, Vintage Books, New York, 1981, p. 261.
7. Fritjof Capra, "The turning point: A new vision of reality," *The Futurist*, December 1982, p. 22–23.
8. Hans Kung, op. cit., p. 123.
9. *Statistical Abstract of the U.S.*, Department of Commerce, Washington, D.C., p. 53.
10. Willis Harman, "Transforming the lifestyle of industrial society," *Optimistic Outlooks*, Global Futures Network, 1982, p. 80.
11. *Publishers Weekly*, April 2, 1982, vol. 221, no. 14, p. 38.
12. Robert Wuthnow, *The Consciousness Reformation*, University of California Press, Berkeley, Calif., 1976, p. 124.
13. Marvin Harris, *America Now*, Simon & Schuster, New York, 1981, p. 173.
14. Barbara Marx Hubbard, "Critical path to an all-win world." *The Futurist*, June 1981, pp. 31–41.
15. Fritjof Capra, op. cit., p. 21.
16. Hans Kung, op. cit., p. 185.
17. Ibid., p. 347.
18. Marilyn Ferguson, *The Aquarian Conspiracy*, J. P. Tarcher, Inc., Los Angeles, 1980, p. 18.
19. Willis Harman, *An Incomplete Guide to the Future*, San Francisco Book Company, San Francisco, 1976, p. 90.
20. Carl H. Madden, "2008," *Across the Board*, The Conference Board, October 1976, p. 18.
21. Daniel Yankelovich, *New Rules*, Random House, New York, 1981, p. 250.
22. Ibid., p. 263.
23. Christopher Lasch, *The Culture of Narcissism*, W. W. Norton & Company, Inc., New York, 1978, p. 235.

24. Robert Nisbet, *History of the Idea of Progress*, Basic Books, Inc., New York, 1980, p. 9.

Chapter 7
From Fantasyland to Fulfillment

1. Amitai Etzioni, *An Immodest Agenda*, McGraw-Hill Book Company, New York, 1983, p. 42.
2. Daniel Yankelovich, *New Rules*, Random House, New York, 1981, p. 85.
3. "Jobs in the 1980s and 1990s," The Public Agenda Foundation and The Aspen Institute for Humanistic Studies, New York, August 1981, executive summary, p. 11.
4. Daniel Yankelovich and John Immerwahr, "Putting the Work Ethic to Work," The Public Agenda Foundation, New York, January 1983 draft paper, p. 23.
5. Harvey Cox, *The Secular City*, The Macmillan Company, revised edition, New York, 1966, p. 164.
6. Marilyn Ferguson, *The Aquarian Conspiracy*, J. P. Tarcher, Inc., Los Angeles, 1980, p. 345.
7. William H. Whyte, Jr., *The Organization Man*, Doubleday Anchor Books edition, Garden City, N.Y., 1956, p. 7.
8. Ibid., p. 10.
9. Maurice F. Strong, "Where Do We Go from Here?," *Optimistic Outlooks*, Global Futures Network, Toronto, 1982, p. 183.

Chapter 8
The Corporation:
Positive and Infinite

1. Thomas J. Peters and Robert H. Waterman, Jr., *In Search of Excellence*, Harper & Row, Publishers, Inc., New York, 1982, p. 103.
2. Kenneth E. Goodpaster and John B. Matthews, Jr., "Can a corporation have a conscience?," *Harvard Business Review*, January–February, 1982, p. 139.
3. Anthony Giddens, *Capitalism and Modern Social Theory*, Cambridge University Press, London, 1971, p. 103.
4. Michael Novak, *The Spirit of Democratic Capitalism*, Simon & Schuster, New York, 1982, p. 181.
5. Andrew M. Greeley, *The Denominational Society*, Scott, Foresman and Company, Glenview, Ill., 1972, p. 134.
6. "Jobs in the 1980s and 1990s," The Public Agenda Foundation and The

Aspen Institute for Humanistic Studies, New York, August 1981, executive summary, p. 3.

7. Eric Trist, "The Evolution of Socio-Technical Systems," Ontario Quality of Working Life Centre paper, Toronto, June 1981, p. 43.

8. "Perspectives on Productivity: A Global View," Sentry Insurance Company, Stevens Point, Wis., 1981, p. 26.

9. Fred T. Allen, speech before a symposium sponsored by the State of Connecticut Department of Education, December 1, 1981.

10. Alvin Toffler, *The Third Wave*, William Morrow and Company, Inc., New York, 1980, pp. 45–46.

11. Perry Pascarella, "The CEOs of the eighties," *Industry Week*, January 7, 1980, p. 83.

Chapter 9
Humanization and Participation

1. Ted Mills, "Human resources—Why the new concern?," *Harvard Business Review*, March–April, 1975, pp. 120–21.

2. Thomas Graham speech at Cleveland Engineering Society, April 24, 1981.

3. Perry Pascarella, *Technology—Fire in a Dark World*, Van Nostrand Reinhold, New York, 1979, p. 83.

4. Douglas McGregor, *The Human Side of Enterprise*, McGraw-Hill Book Company, New York, 1960, p. 245.

5. Frederick Herzberg, *Work and the Nature of Man*, World Publishing Company, Cleveland, Ohio, 1966, p. x.

6. Robert Schrank, *Ten Thousand Working Days*, The MIT Press, Cambridge Mass., 1978, p. 242.

7. William G. Scott and David K. Hart, *Organizational America*, Houghton Mifflin Company, Boston, 1979, p. 74.

8. Frederick Herzberg, "Participation is not a motivator," *Industry Week*, September 4, 1978, pp. 39–41.

9. Douglas McGregor, op. cit., p. 46.

10. Kenichi Ohmae, *The Mind of the Strategist*, McGraw-Hill Book Company, New York, 1982, p. 217.

11. Ibid., p. 207.

12. William Ouchi, *Theory Z*, Addison-Wesley Publishing Company, Reading, Mass., 1981.

13. Jerome Rosow, "A new direction for labor: Quality of working life," *World of Work Report*, Work in America Institute, Scarsdale, N.Y., March 1982, p. 19.

14. Kenichi Ohmae, op. cit., p. 206.

15. Marilyn Ferguson, *The Aquarian Conspiracy*, J. P. Tarcher, Inc., Los Angeles, 1980, p. 129.

16. Douglas McGregor, op. cit., p. 49.
17. Alvin Toffler, *The Third Wave*, William Morrow and Company, Inc., New York, 1980, pp. 62–76.

Chapter 10
Coming Alive at Work

1. Michael Maccoby, *The Leader*, Simon & Schuster, New York, 1981, p. 216.
2. William G. Scott and David K. Hart, *Organizational America*, Houghton Mifflin Company, Boston, 1979, p. 31.
3. Alvin Toffler, *Preview and Premises*, William Morrow and Company, Inc., New York, 1983, p. 38.
4. James J. O'Toole, "What kind of work works in a slow-growth era?" *Industry Week*, June 9, 1980, p. 87.
5. Barbara Marx Hubbard, *The Hunger of Eve*, Stackpole Books, Harrisburg, Pa., 1976, p. 177.
6. William H. Whyte, Jr., *The Organization Man*, Doubleday Anchor Books edition, Garden City, N.Y., 1956, p. 14.
7. Ibid., pp. 50–51.
8. Alvin Toffler, *The Third Wave*, William Morrow and Company, Inc., New York, 1980, p. 219.
9. Richard E. Walton, "New perspectives on the world of work," *Human Relations*, vol. 35, November 12, 1982, p. 1079.
10. Ibid., pp. 1078–79.
11. Michael Novak, *The Spirit of Democratic Capitalism*, Simon & Schuster, New York, 1982, p. 80.

Chapter 11
The Quality of Management

1. Perry Pascarella, "Management doesn't 'think productivity'," *Industry Week*, February 18, 1980, pp. 18–19.
2. Robert H. Hayes and William J. Abernathy, "Managing our way to economic decline," *Harvard Business Review*, July–August 1980, pp. 67–77.
3. Mary Cunningham, "Corporate culture determines productivity," *Industry Week*, May 4, 1981, p. 84.
4. Kenichi Ohmae, *The Mind of the Strategist*, McGraw-Hill Book Company, New York, 1982, pp. 137–38.
5. William Abernathy, Kim Clark, and Alan Kantrow, *Industrial Renaissance*, Basic Books, Inc., New York, 1983, p. 118.
6. Douglas McGregor, *The Human Side of Enterprise*, McGraw-Hill Book Company, New York, 1960, pp. 46–47.

7. Frederick Herzberg, "Management of motivators," *Industry Week*, February 15, 1971, p. 54.

Chapter 12
The Purpose Is Quality

1. Ernest Becker, *The Denial of Death*, The Free Press, New York, 1973, p. 6.
2. "Industrial psychology on the line," *Psychology Today*, July 1978, p. 69.

Chapter 13
The Soul of Management

1. Perry Pascarella, *Industry Week's Guide to Tomorrow's Executive: Humanagement in the Future Corporation*, Van Nostrand Reinhold, New York, 1981, p. 15.
2. "The Connecticut Mutual Life Report on American Values in the '80s." Connecticut Mutual Life Insurance Co., Hartford, Conn., 1981, pp. 214–26.
3. Ibid.
4. Ibid., 194.
5. Michael Maccoby, *The Leader*, Simon & Schuster, New York, 1981, p. 231.
6. Frederick Herzberg, "Humanities: practical management education," *Industry Week*, September 29, 1980, pp. 69–72.
7. Perry Pascarella, "The CEOs of the eighties," *Industry Week*, January 7, 1980, pp. 75–83.
8. Ibid.
9. Michael Maccoby, op. cit., p. 19.
10. Marilyn Ferguson, *The Aquarian Conspiracy*, J. P. Tarcher, Inc., Los Angeles, 1980, p. 340.
11. "Chief Executive Officer Survey," conducted by The Roper Organization Inc. for Warburg Paribas Becker, June 15, 1982.
12. Abraham Maslow, *Religions, Values, and Peak Experiences*, Viking Compass edition, New York, 1970, p. xii.

Index